SUSAN SAYER

Lent for the whole church community

- A Shrove Tuesday party
- All-age ideas for Holy Week
- 'Open church' days in Lent
- Kite-making
- Making a prayer trail
- Telling the Good Friday story

kevin mayhew

First published in 2003 by

KEVIN MAYHEW LTD
Buxhall, Stowmarket, Suffolk, IP14 3BW
E-mail: info@kevinmayhewltd.com

KINGSGATE PUBLISHING INC
1000 Pannell Street, Suite G, Columbia, MO 65201
E-mail: sales@kingsgatepublishing.com

9 8 7 6 5 4 3 2 1 0

ISBN 184417 179 5
Catalogue No 1500668

Cover design and drawings by Angela Selfe
Edited by Katherine Laidler
Typesetting by Louise Selfe
Printed in Great Britain

Contents

Catching the mood of Lent

*'I was going to give up sweets for Lent, but I couldn't find any Lent,
so I had to go back to the sweets.'*

Even today quite a lot of people know of Lent – usually as some rather archaic slimming programme, an old traditional ritual of giving something up for a while to prove you can. Shrove Tuesday is now Pancake Day, Good Friday is a quaint name for the home-decorating Bank Holiday, and hot cross buns are available all year round. Lent isn't one of those Christian seasons that has leaked out into mainstream living.

The advantage of this is that the church community is not engaged in an ongoing battle to haul Lent back to its roots. There is no battle. Lent is largely a well-kept secret. The disadvantage is that for the church community there is quite a freak factor about keeping Lent and Holy Week. We get noticed for being different. So what is this season of Lent all about? Where did a tradition of giving up sweets or sugar in our tea spring from?

The English name of this Lent season is linked with the lengthening spring days of the northern hemisphere, and that is because it was originally the time of heart-searching preparation for those approaching their Easter baptism.

With an expectant mood of preparation in the air, there are strong links with Jesus' own preparation for his ministry, a 40-day process of prayer and fasting spent wrestling with how best to proclaim the kingdom. 'Wrestling', because whenever we move forwards in our faith journey the temptations come thick and fast to throw us off course, water down our commitment or edge us out of a healthy relationship with God.

And in his humanness Jesus knew the full force of all that. One of the most encouraging things for us is the knowledge that Jesus knows exactly what it's like to have powerful temptations battering at you, whispering possibilities that sound close enough to the truth to be plausible, but are really like 'wolves in sheep's clothing'.

The day before Lent is Shrove Tuesday, the day when you confessed your sins and were shriven, or forgiven, so as to start Lent with a clean conscience. With the time of fasting from luxuries ahead, this Tuesday was also the time to use up all your fine food in a feast, which is where the carnival (or 'good-bye to meat') festival comes from, and the Mardi Gras (or 'Greasy Tuesday').

In contrast, Ash Wednesday, the first day of Lent, is an occasion for collectively facing up to the truth of who we really are – created, human and mortal. Our own mortality and time-bound existence opens our eyes to the eternal and always-present nature of God, so that we recognise more fully the generosity of God's grace, loving mercy and forgiveness. Together as Church we can use this whole Lent season of soul searching creatively. We wrestle with the problem of evil and our fractured relationship with God, tracing the human story through scripture, and always aware of Jesus' power to heal and restore.

Is any of this suitable for the younger members of the Body of Christ? Or should we leave them out of all this? If we do, and then suddenly plunge them into Easter, I think we sell them pitifully short. As full members of the Body, our youngest and oldest alike are an organic part of the love community which is Church. We need to explore these areas of our common human experience together as family. We learn from one another, and we learn by engaging in the process of looking out for one another's needs along the way.

Like Advent, the Church's colour for this season is purple, right up to Palm Sunday, because we are exploring the rich but dark areas of our humanity. Many church communities will meet in small groups during the weekdays of Lent to be disciplined and to pray, and for some odd reason this practice has not often included the children. But of course it is perfectly possible, and of great value, to make such groups available for all the ages. In this book there are family meal-based activities for use at home, and individual copiable worksheets, with weekly gathered sessions for churches and school groups.

Traditionally the church building is often bare of flowers during Lent, and fasting from luxuries or addressing a particular weakness is also practised. The mood is of a longing for God's healing and guidance in our lives and in the whole human condition, so it is really all about holiness and humility. There are suggestions in this book for working this out in a practical way through a community 'grown-from-seed' Easter garden, for instance, and through pilgrimage.

The pared-down simplicity and earthing of our faith journey doesn't mean that Lent is a season of long faces and self-flagellation. There is a wholesome maturity about setting a season for facing deep issues, and an excitement about the way God works in us to heal and transform, whatever our age. In our churches we need to provide space and opportunity for people to meet honestly with God and allow the healing and transforming to happen. That may well mean the church being open and available on a 'drop-in' basis, and the suggested Lent open-church days offer you help in how to go about providing for this.

In every season of the year, each Sunday also retains the affirming joy of resurrection, of course, and on Mothering Sunday – the fourth in Lent – we celebrate our thankfulness for practical loving care in all relationships, and in particular our human parenting, and God's parenting of us. What better seasonal landscape than Lent to host such celebration. Ideas for Mothering Sunday worship are provided, bearing in mind that this is often a time when people come who are not regular church attenders.

By the fifth Sunday of Lent, the shadow of the cross is more sharply defined, and we prepare to get back into 'real time' so as to walk with Jesus through that last week of his life on earth before crucifixion. This starts with Palm Sunday, and the colour changes from purple to red, the colour of blood and sacrifice. The week is sometimes known as Holy Week.

Instinctively we want our buildings to express this heightened awareness of Christ's saving death, and many churches install a bare wooden cross as a focus for this time. There are no flowers, as if we are fasting. In some churches any statues are covered up from the fifth Sunday onwards, so that nothing distracts from the stark reality of the Passion. It is a week of spiritually journeying together, for Spring Harvest or Iona; for a parish pilgrimage around the church or further afield; for daily gathered prayer, or a community commitment to read a complete Gospel during the week.

On Palm Sunday we enact in our worship the procession into Jerusalem, tasting the bitter-sweet emotions of the crowd's hosannas and their call for Jesus' execution. This was an all-age crowd if ever there was one, with the children's voices recorded as ringing out with a truth the authorities found offensive. If you haven't tried it before, do consider having a procession through the streets on this day as part of the worship, with waving branches and streamers. You could even have a donkey.

Passover meals are an excellent way of entering into the whole story as a whole community, and there is a script provided for this. Often these meals are held on Maundy Thursday – the day of Jesus' last supper with his disciples – either as an extended Eucharist or as a separate Agape meal. Increasingly on Maundy Thursday churches of all traditions are valuing the idea of a garden set up in the church as a focus for watching and praying on a rota basis during the evening and night.

Finally, Good Friday is one of those occasions in the year when there is a real longing for unity, as we share this day together. A walk in the way of the cross might involve all local churches, working together on planning each stopping place along the route to reflect on the meaning of the cross, or staging a shared dramatised telling of the Good Friday story, and there are ideas to help with such an event. Such whole community events are wonderful opportunities for God to work on healing our divisions, not just across denominations and traditions of worship but also across age-group barriers. Good Friday ends by looking forward to the hope and joy of the resurrection, as the Lent season draws to a close.

A Shrove Tuesday party

It's quite fun to stage some kind of carnival or festive party for all ages on Shrove Tuesday, as part of our preparation for travelling through Lent together. You could start the evening with a short reflective time of penitence – a suggested liturgy is given below – and then launch into a festive party atmosphere with pancakes, of course, silly games and dancing. Pick a theme (princes and princesses, Bible characters, book characters, film characters, soap characters, medieval banquet, Madame Tussaud's, etc.) and invite people to come dressed up. Remind everyone about the Lent journey and as they go give out the appropriate sheets for the first week of it.

A liturgy of penitence and reconciliation

Set up beforehand an atmosphere of beauty and reverence, with lots of candles standing on mirrors or foil for the reflections, flowers and draped white cloth – muslin or silky fabric. If you have a wide, flat bowl of water, place floating candles and a few flower heads in it. Or have one of those indoor fountains so that there is the gentle sound of running water. No service sheet is necessary.

Put up large BE STILL signs and have some quiet music – flute or harp, perhaps, Taizé or worship songs. Make sure the little ones are where they can see the beauty and candlelight well, and, as far as possible, one to one with a young person or adult.

Sing (or listen to) something that reminds you all of God's great love for you. For instance:
- The Lord's my shepherd, I'll not want (Crimmond)
- Jesu, the very thought of thee
- What a friend I've found
- So freely

The priest or minister says something like this:
It is true – God loves each of us, and is here with us now, as we worship together. Let's think for a minute. Is there anything we need to tell Jesus about? Is there anything you have done which you know was unkind or wrong or selfish or dishonest? Are there good things you could have done and said but chose not to? What kind of person are you at the moment in God's eyes? Rich or poor? Healthy or in need of the healing touch of God's forgiveness?

In the quietness, tell Jesus what is on your mind and in your heart. Tell Jesus how you're sorry and long to be forgiven.

During this time of collective penitence, either have silence or quiet music.

8

Priest or minister:
The Lord hears the cry of our hearts. To every person who comes to him in sorrow for sin, knowing their need of forgiveness, Jesus says these words: 'Your sins are forgiven. Go in peace!'

Sing something that lets you express your thanks and sense of freedom, such as:

- I'm accepted, I'm forgiven
- I am a new creation
- Give thanks with a grateful heart
- Amazing grace
- Father, we love you

Share a sign of God's peace with one another, and say the Grace together:
May the grace of our Lord Jesus Christ,
and the love of God,
and the fellowship of the Holy Spirit,
be with us all evermore.
Amen.

And now, the party!

Daily prayers for Lent

'Watch and pray, so that you don't fall into temptation.'

These prayers can be copied and distributed at the beginning of Lent, as age-appropriate. Committing ourselves as a whole community to a 'morning, meals and night' prayer pattern is both simple and actually very powerful, binding us together in God and keeping our spiritual eyes and ears open. It is good practice for all ages of Christ followers to pray in a regular way like this.

Morning prayers

Thank you, Father, for the gift of life.
Thank you for the gift of this new spring day.
I want to live it in your company,
attentive to your will
and ready to act on your command.
During this Lent
teach me more about who you are
and who I am,
so that my life may become
a daily song of praise.
Amen.

(To the tune of 'Half a pound of tuppenny rice')
In the sun and showers of rain
all the flowers are showing.
In the love and power of God
our love is growing.

Thank you, God, for making us grow
big and strong and loving.
In the love and power of God
our love is growing.

Today and now is the only time that I can live in your company.
Today and now is the only time that I can love.
Today might be the only day that I can pay my debts and forgive.
Today might be the only day that I can help,
or stay and listen, or speak out against injustice.
Lord of all time and eternity,
give me the grace to live each moment to the full.
Amen.

Give me the grace to live more simply;
give me the grace to simply live,
rich in your love and trusting in your mercy.
Amen.

As these Lent days lengthen,
help me to grow
more and more responsive
to your love and your call.
Amen.

(To the tune of 'Row, row, row your boat')
Grow, grow, grow in love,
grow in love today.
Listen to Jesus and do what he says
each and every day.

Saying Grace before meals

God's good earth has given us food.
Blessed be God for ever.

Thank you for feeding us, Holy God.
As we eat this food for our bodies,
so feed us also with your grace and love
sufficient for the work you would have us do.
Amen.

We cannot live by bread alone
but by every word that comes
from the mouth of God.
May we feed on both
with thankfulness.
Amen.

Bless this food
that it may provide us
with all the energy and strength we need
to do your will.
Amen.

(To the tune of 'When the saints go marching in')
Oh as we eat our daily bread,
oh as we eat our daily bread,
we want to thank our heavenly Father
for giving us our daily bread.

Night prayers

Safe in the shadow of your wings, O Lord,
we settle ourselves to sleep.
Watch over us and bless us through this night.
Amen.

I come to the end of the day.
It is time to fold up
the things I have completed
and the things I have been unable to do.
Let me lay them down in peace.
Father, give me the grace
to forgive any who have wronged or hurt me today.
Forgive those things I regret
and of which I am ashamed,
and heal me.
Thank you for the times I have been able
to act justly,
love with mercy
and walk humbly with you, my God.
Thank you for the opportunities the day has given
to practise patience, humility,
forgiveness, kindness and compassion.
So now, as I lie down to sleep,
into your hands, O Lord, I commit my spirit.
Amen.

(To the tune of 'Twinkle, twinkle, little star')
Now the stars are shining bright,
Jesus, keep us safe tonight.
Thank you for your loving care
for your children everywhere.
May we shine with love like you
in all we think and say and do.
Amen.

Glory to God
who always was, always will be,
and is now, as I pray.
Your grace is sufficient for me.
Your love is all I need.
Amen.

Lenten eating . . . and Lenten fasting

Lent is a particularly good opportunity to practise generous giving, both individually and as a church community, sharing the resources of our world, noticing needs and addressing them. Can I make a plea for children to be included in this – giving not what an adult has just passed to them, but out of money they have saved from their own pocket money. It often helps us to give generously if we link our giving with some practical imaginative experience, especially as much of our mean-spiritedness is born of ignorance about the practical horrors of living without enough, since we are often so used to having enough ourselves.

- **Water fetching, water tasting.** No doubt generations to come will find it extraordinary and shocking that the wealthier Christians in the West did so little to address such a basic and urgent need as worldwide availability of clean water. If a Lent project focuses on providing a community with that basic essential of clean water, the need might be highlighted by staging a water tasting, or a water carrying, from one end of the High Street to the other, together with a display of images to explain the every-day problems of those whose water source is some distance from home. Tell the local press about it, write a piece to catch their imagination so they come and publicise the work with photographs and headlines, and involve local schools.

- **'Manna? What's this?'** If the Lent project is addressing the needs of a particular country or culture, collect some recipes and give them out for families to try cooking at home, together with an appropriate prayer for the project. Charities such as Tear Fund, Christian Aid, ActionAid, CAFOD and Oxfam all provide excellent suggestions to use.

- **Share the meal, share the pain.** To encourage the community discipline of living more simply, and sharing our world's resources more fairly, have a weekly 'lentils', 'rice and vegetables' or 'porridge' meal – either after church on a Sunday, or in a drop-in way on a Saturday lunch time, with donations invited for passing on to those who have to survive on very little.

- **Stones into bread.** The 'stones into bread' temptation gives us a good indication of what the ordinary loaves looked like in Jesus' culture. Have a go at making some stone-shaped loaves, and before eating them, place them among some pebble stones as a focus for prayer in church, in the classroom or at home, together with the words of Jesus' temptations in the desert. As each person picks up a small loaf to eat, they replace the loaf with some money which can be donated to a Lent appeal.

- **Make some hot cross buns.** At one time bakers made a cross on all their buns – it was a sign that they had been prayed over. Gradually people started to leave the crosses off – except on Good Friday. It's fun to make your own hot cross buns for a change, and they can be as fruity and spicy as you like. The crosses on them can either be cut with a knife or made from thin strips of ready-made shortcrust pastry. Make sure you have washed your hands thoroughly before you start baking. Give some of them away.

- **Have a stone soup meal**. Invite everyone coming to bring one vegetable – a potato, a leek, a carrot, an onion, herbs or whatever. You will also need a clean stone, a large saucepan and stock cubes to taste. One person tells the 'stone soup' story (it's on page 87). Then play some worship music to sing along to as everyone prepares the soup together, first boiling the water with the stone in it, and then cleaning, chopping, grating and adding all the other ingredients, so everyone contributes and has a stir. While the soup cooks, everyone helps to lay the table and make it look beautiful. Have on the table the collection plate for giving to your Lent charity, with pictures and information about it around the room. Say or sing Grace together, and enjoy the stone soup with bread, which can be broken and passed round during the Grace.

- **Family fasting.** Consider working together as a family to give up something collectively. It might be opting for a supermarket's basic range of products rather than the usual brand names, for instance, or having a boot sale of family clutter. Make a celebration of the giving, so that it becomes a fun and exciting event to watch the collecting jar filling up, reaching the target amount for a particular donation. It doesn't have to involve a financial gift, of course – you could each try fasting from a habit, so that whenever you go to do what you usually do, the fasting reminds you to touch base with God.

- **Not what you expect.** One of the things we find as we follow Jesus is that God's ways are not always what we might expect. That's why we have to keep flexible in spirit! Not-what-you-expect food might be things like tomatoes included in a fruit salad, green custard (just add some food colouring), dessert served before the first course, 'fish' made out of sausage meat, or orange icing tasting of mint. A table arrangement might be of mixed flowers, fruit and watercress, and ice cubes have flowers frozen inside them.

An all-age Lent journey: 'Who am I?'

This is a Lent journey we can all travel together as church, whatever our age or shoe size. The same areas are explored right across the age range each week, and celebrated each Sunday in an exhibition or display, to which everyone has contributed. This means that we are all helping one another along the way, and learning from one another's insights. The only leader for everyone is Jesus, the one we Christians have chosen to follow, and the aim of the journey is to discover more about who God is and more about who we are.

There are separate sheets for Babies and Toddlers, Children, Youth and Adults. Copy the appropriate sheets week by week for everyone in the church, and appoint a mixed-age team to display the work Sunday by Sunday. Include a copy of each sheet in the displays.

People can work through the material in small groups, in households, tutor groups or in friendship groups, as part of a weekly club, or on their own. The weekly activities are deliberately flexible and open-ended so that no one is left out.

The weekly display

The display needs to be in the place you meet for refreshments before or after church on Sundays. Publicise the displays and encourage people to look round them each week. Or make them a part of the worship, by giving space for people to look around just before or during the service, while music is playing. The displays become focuses for prayer and openness to God.

Throughout Lent the display grows and becomes a visual 'logbook' of a shared spiritual journey. Have the display available at the AGM of the Church council which is often held at this time of year.

Week 1: Human and mortal

Babies and Toddlers
(with a little help from their friends)

This week's message for you from God . . .

Before I
formed you in the womb
I knew you!

Things to do this week . . .

1. Look at some pictures of when you were a new baby (or even before you were born). How have you changed?
2. Try out the clever things you have learnt to do. (Roll over, hold something and let it go, smile, eat, drink, yawn, crawl, walk, talk, listen, hug, give, etc.)
3. Look in a mirror.
4. Collect some twigs with buds on them and put them in water. Watch for when the buds open.
5. Draw a picture of you and your family.

Week 1: Human and mortal

Children
(with a little help from their friends)

This week's message for you from God . . .

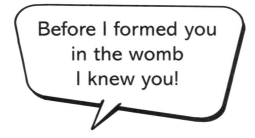

This is a picture of me

Who am I? Am I a goldfish? Am I a mountain? Am I a cat?
NO! I am a Human Being.

- How tall are you?

....

- What colour are your eyes?

 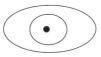

- Try recording your voice and listening to it. Does it sound like you or not?
- Choose a piece of paper in your favourite colour. Make some fingerprints on it using an inkpad or colouring your finger with a black felt-tip pen.

YOU ARE THE ONLY HUMAN BEING
WHO HAS THIS FINGERPRINT! YOU ARE UNIQUE!

- Practise writing your signature. When you're happy with it, sign here!

....

Week 1: Human and mortal

Youth

This week's message for you from God . . .

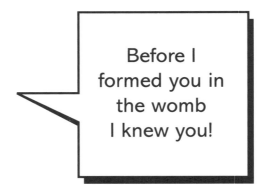

Part of the amazing thing about being human is *knowing* we're human. Being, and also being aware of Being. We've got these incredible minds that can sort out the world around us and make some kind of sense out of it. And part of that is that each person is unique. For instance, no one else thinks or reacts or imagines exactly like you do. No one else knows exactly what it's like to be you – apart from God, that is. Sometimes we don't even understand ourselves, do we? I reckon we spend a lifetime discovering who we really are.

- Play around with your name or initials using different fonts, colours and some clip art, if you like working on a computer, or make a collage picture with the letters cut out from newspapers and magazines and adverts, to make a statement about your-self and who you have discovered yourself to be so far.

- Read Psalm 139:1-6, 13-18
- Spend a bit of time on your own with God, sitting really still and letting it sink in that God is the one who knows, loves and understands you best.

Week 1: Human and mortal

Adults

This week's message for you from God . . .

> Before I formed
> you in the womb
> I knew you!

One of the most important things about being human is that we're in the 'begin and end' dimension of Time. We know we start at the fusion of a male sperm and a female egg, and that we develop from a single cell into a Human Being, capable of an immense range of skills, great mental agility and deep relationships.

And then, at some point – we die.

In spite of all that growth and mastery, it all finishes when the pulse stops and the breathing ends. Ever since humans have been humans, we've hated being mortal – felt somehow cheated by the brutal fact of death.

So to be human is to be able to know the great fullness of life and also to be aware of how trapped we are by time and mortality.

- Are there any advantages of being mortal, do you think?
- What difference does death make to our approach to living?
- What is 'being human' at its best?
- What is 'being human' at its worst?

This week's assignment . . .

- Read Psalm 139:1-6, 13-18.
- Choose a piece of coloured paper and write, draw or stick on it any words and pictures which express what it means to be Human and Mortal.

Week 2: Created

Babies and Toddlers
(with a little help from their friends)

This week's message for you from God . . .

> It is God who made us and we are his; we are his people and the sheep of his pasture.

God made the stars and the sun, the earth where we live, and the air that we breathe. He made water and all the plants and animals. And he made us – you and me. God loves what he has made very much.

Things to do this week . . .

1. Enjoy making something! (A tower of bricks, shadows with your fingers, a junk model, or something to eat, perhaps.)
2. What different animals and plants can you spot this week? Draw them here.

Thank you, God, for making such a lovely world for us to live in!

3. Collect pictures of animals and plants and people and stars and stick them all over a box. Tie a ribbon round it and a tag which says:

'With love from God x x'

Week 2: Created

Children
(with a little help from their friends)

This week's message for you from God . . .

> It is God who made us and we are his; we are his people and the sheep of his pasture.

(Shut your eyes and cover them with your hands.)

In the beginning it was dark and empty.

(Open your eyes and look around.)

God said, 'Let there be light!' And there was light. God made sky and water, the sun, moon and stars, all the animals and plants, the birds and the insects.
And then . . .

(Raise your hands and look at them.)

God made people. He saw that what he had made was very good.
God loves the world and God loves us.

Things to do this week . . .

- Get some modelling clay or dough and make a model of a person or a plant or an animal.
- Make a place for your model to live – like this:

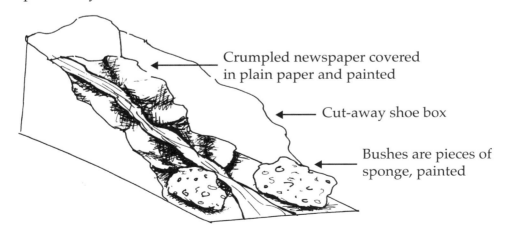

Crumpled newspaper covered in plain paper and painted

Cut-away shoe box

Bushes are pieces of sponge, painted

'You gave me a heart and you gave me a smile,
you gave me Jesus and you made me your child,
and I just want to thank you for making me ME!'

Week 2: Created

Youth

This week's message for you from God . . .

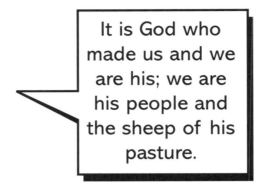

It is God who made us and we are his; we are his people and the sheep of his pasture.

Some people think that this universe just happened. I used to think that too. But it's a bit like the possibility of a monkey with a computer accidentally writing the works of Shakespeare – possible, but not all that likely, really. When I realised quite how precise are the details needed for creation to happen, I started to wonder if I just didn't want to believe the more obvious explanation – that this universe was all carefully and lovingly planned.

'God' is the name we give to the Being who loves our universe into existence. God builds into his creation the possibility for growth and development, and even the possibility for close relationship with the Maker himself.

To think about this week . . .

- Knowing we are made means knowing there is someone who wanted to make us. How does that change our attitude to life?

To do this week . . .

- Read Acts 17:24-28 (It's how Paul explains creation to the people in Athens during the first century AD, but it still makes sense today.)
- Express the moment of creation in art or poetry *or*
- Draw a diagram of the solar system, gravity, or the molecular structure of water.

Week 2: Created

Adults

This week's message for you from God . . .

> It is God who made us and we are his; we are his people and the sheep of his pasture.

'Created' has a very different ring from just 'happened', hasn't it? Created suggests some kind of relationship between the Maker who makes, and what is made. You can't 'create' without thinking carefully and imaginatively, and wanting to express yourself in what you do.

So if it is true that our universe, with all its variety and detail and possibility, is an expression of the Maker (whom we call God), then God must have loved all this into being. God must have loved US into being.

Well, then, how does it feel to belong to a Personal Maker? How does it feel to look around at all the rest of creation and know that it isn't accidental but lovingly and reverently held and cherished and given space to adapt and change?

This week's assignment . . .

- Read Acts 17:24-28 (It's how Paul explains creation to the people in Athens during the first century AD, but it still makes sense today.)
- Express the relationship between Maker and creation in art or poetry.
- Take time to look closely at a tree or the clouds, or the sea, as the works of God's hand.

Week 3: In the likeness of God

Babies and Toddlers
(with a little help from their friends)

This week's message for you from God . . .

> You have been made in my likeness.

One day when Jesus was walking along, the grown-ups were arguing about which of them was most important. Jesus stood a little child in the middle of them and said, 'Whoever welcomes a little child like this, welcomes me.' (Little children and babies are very good at showing grown-ups how to love God.)

Things to do this week . . .

- Have someone you love swinging you backwards and forwards (either on a swing or in their arms) while you both sing 'He's got the whole world in his hands'. (God loves us and looks after us, and we look after each other and love each other.)
- Make some coloured sweets or pieces of fruit into a picture of a person or a face on a plate. (God likes making people, too.)
- Sort out some coloured sweets into their different colours. Take turns choosing a colour and eating a sweet. (God likes sharing and working with his friends, too!)
- Find a feather, watch it falling through the air, then stroke your cheek with it. Isn't it soft! (God is gentle and kind. And God thinks about things.)
- Make a paper crown and wear it as God's child.

I AM GOD'S CHILD. GOD MADE ME AND LOVES ME.

Week 3: In the likeness of God

Children
(with a little help from their friends)

This week's message for you from God . . .

You have
been made in my
likeness.

God is God and you are a human being. But in lots of ways God made us like him.

- God loves, and we can love.

  (Who do you love?)

- God thinks, and we can think.

  (Think about something you like doing. Think about how a chocolate Easter egg might be made.)

- God imagines, and we can imagine.

  (Imagine a blue elephant with green spots. Imagine being able to fly.)

- God chooses, and we can choose.

  (Which do you like best – pizza or chicken nuggets? Are you going to help someone today or hurt them?)

Things to do this week . . .

- Whenever you're not sure about what's right, THINK: 'God made me like himself.' THEN ASK YOURSELF: 'What would God want me to do?'

- Get a sheet of paper and fold it into four. Draw a circle in the middle and write in it 'AM I?' In each quarter, write the words 'GOD IS'. Choose four words from the list below (or choose your own words) so you have four sentences describing God.

Word list:

LOVING   CAREFUL   TRUTHFUL   FAITHFUL   FORGIVING   KIND

GENEROUS   BRAVE   TRUSTWORTHY   GENTLE   HAPPY   FAIR

Week 3: In the likeness of God

Youth

This week's message for you from God . . .

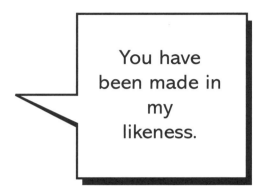

You have been made in my likeness.

It says in Genesis 1:27: 'So God created humankind in his image, in the image of God he created them; male and female he created them.' Which means that if we take a look at what *we* are like at our best, we should get an idea of what God is like. He must be like that, only much more so, because he's not just 'in the image', but the Person himself. It's like looking at a reflection in a river to find out what the riverside buildings are like.

Let's look at our humanness again. We can think, imagine and choose; we can feel and respond emotionally; and we can express ourselves in words and actions. Take that into the God-dimension (the actual riverside buildings rather than the reflections), and what you come up with is some quite deep things about the nature of God – who is the imaginative thoughtful Creator, who is Jesus, the real life expression of God in human form, and who is the warm and life-giving Holy Spirit. It makes you think.

Things to do this week . . .

- Notice people's behaviour this week (including your own) and notice when they behave in a 'godly' (in God's likeness) kind of way. You may be in for some surprises.
- On a sheet of paper, write down what you'd expect a 'godly' person to be like in the ordinary practical world you live in.

Week 3: In the likeness of God

Adults

This week's message for you from God . . .

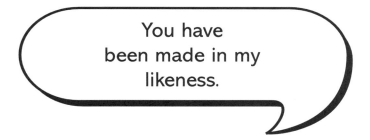

You have been made in my likeness.

We're so used to seeing our image and likeness in a reflection that we don't always recognise a photo of us as right – the reality seems the wrong way round! Some people think that rather than God making us in *his* image, we have actually invented God in *our* image. I used to think that.

But meeting God through the personal relationship of Jesus makes it all clearer, because in Jesus we can see what it really means to be fully human and fully in the image of God. The creative, healing and restoring nature of Jesus expresses the nature of the very Being who would love a universe into existence, making himself vulnerable so that love could be possible.

The more we get to know God, the more we shall get to understand about ourselves, because we are made in God's image and likeness, not he in ours. That's why we feel at our most deeply comfortable and fulfilled not when we're indulging our selfishness but when we sense we are living in harmony with God.

This week's assignment . . .

- Read Genesis 1:26-27 and Psalm 8:3-5.
- Think of a sheet of paper as a tombstone and write on it what you would like to be said about your life.

Week 4: Chosen and called

Babies and Toddlers
(with a little help from their friends)

This week's message for you from God . . .

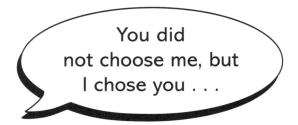

The prophet Samuel was still a very young child when God called him. Many people have felt God calling them when they were very little – perhaps because young children are often better than adults at being open to God! God doesn't need to talk with a voice. He's closer than that. He calls good, loving ideas straight into us.

Things to do this week . . .

- Play this kind of hide and seek. One person hides. The other calls out, 'Where are you?' The hidden person calls back, 'Here I am!' The seeker follows the voice to find where they are. (With babies, play 'Peep-bo', or they can join in by pairing up with an adult.)
- Do some dressing up as all kinds of different people.
- Take a photo of the favourite costume or bring it along for the display. Mount the photo with a question mark, or cut out and pin a question mark on to the costume.

Week 4: Chosen and called

Children
(with a little help from their friends)

This week's message for you from God . . .

You did
not choose me, but
I chose you . . .

Have you ever been chosen for a special job? Like carrying the register, collecting pencils or leading the other children out to playtime?
Act it out and see if we can guess what job it is.

Jesus needed someone who was at (Porters Grange) school . . .
That's ME!
Someone who had just learnt to (ride a bike) . . .
That's ME!
Someone who had (one big brother and one baby sister) . . .
That's ME!
Someone who was good at (cheering people up) . . .
That's ME!
Jesus has chosen and called YOU to follow him!
Are you too old? *NO!* Are you too young? *NO!*
You are just right!

Things to do this week . . .

- Notice whenever God calls and chooses you to work with him. You will be walking through the week together.
- Every morning say to Jesus, 'Hello Jesus, here I am!'
- Read about Jesus calling Peter and Andrew. It's in Matthew 4:18, 19, or you may have the story in a children's Bible.
- Make a picture of Jesus calling the two fishermen in their boat.

Week 4: Chosen and called

Youth

This week's message for you from God . . .

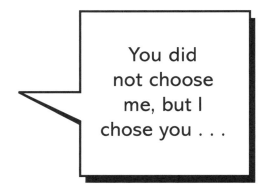

We're made like God, so we have freedom of choice. (If we weren't free to choose, we wouldn't be equipped to love – because you can't ever be *made* to love, can you?) But God knows that loving will make us our most humanly fulfilled – even though loving does often mean we get hurt.

Something has nudged you into doing this Lent course, where you're taking God seriously and thinking about the big questions that people often try to avoid. God has chosen you and is calling deep into your personality to follow Jesus and walk with him through your life. But Jesus respects you and always leaves you the choice – whether to ignore his call, or whether to say, 'Here I am, Jesus. The answer's yes. I *do* want to come with you. I want to get to know you better. Welcome into my life!'

Things to do this week . . .

- Think over God's call to you. It won't always be easy travelling with Jesus, but it will be challenging and very rewarding. It's certainly never dull! Go somewhere on your own and respond as you choose, with the free will God has given you.
- Live through the week in both dimensions at once – walking down the road *and* walking with Jesus. See what happens.
- Express how that feels, in art, music or poetry.

Week 4: Chosen and called

Adults

This week's message for you from God . . .

> You did
> not choose me, but
> I chose you . . .

Often people ask why God didn't make the world and humans differently. Why didn't he make us so we always choose what is good? Then all the suffering could be avoided. It sounds sensible and kind. But if we were only equipped to choose good, it wouldn't really be choosing, would it? And God respects us more than that. He knows it's dangerous and allows himself to be caught up in the vulnerability. But the cost is worth it, if it means we are capable of the very highest human adventure – loving. Loving our Maker in a real relationship, and loving one another in the sense of being community. We're not always very good at it, and we retire hurt at the first hurdle without letting God teach us the delicate skills of community living.

But that is what God is calling us into – a love community of Jesus-followers, who can help the world by being this healing and forgiving pulse at the very centre of ordinary, messy life.

Do we use our God-given freedom of choice to hear the call and respond to it? Or do we ignore it and hope it will go away? Or do we kid ourselves that it means something more comfortable?

This week's assignment . . .

- Find somewhere quiet to think over what it really means to be chosen and called by Jesus. Respond to his call simply and honestly.
- Live through the week in both dimensions at once – walking down the road *and* walking with Jesus. See what happens.
- Express how that feels, in art, music or poetry.

Week 5: Not servants but friends

Babies and Toddlers
(with a little help from their friends)

This week's message for you from God . . .

> Live in me
> as I live in you.

Servants are just told what to do. But friends like spending time together. Friends like to have fun and play together. And Jesus calls us to be his friends.

Things to do this week . . .

- Get into the habit of talking with Jesus in the morning, before you eat, and just before you go to sleep.
- Help make a 'Jesus is my friend' mobile.

You will need:
Drinking straws
Strong cotton
Thin card
Pens and scissors

What you do . . .
1. Make the cards
2. Hang them on the straws with cotton

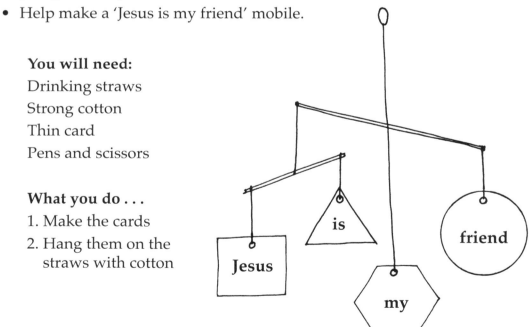

- Get a children's Bible and keep it by your bed, so you can hear about Jesus and get to know him better.

Week 5: Not servants but friends

Children
(with a little help from their friends)

This week's message for you from God . . .

Live in me
as I live in you.

'Scrub the floor!' 'Carry my shopping!' 'Make me a drink!' 'Clear up the mess I've made!'

Jesus says, 'Don't treat each other like that. It's bossy and rude. I don't treat you as servants but as my dear friends. Think of me as your friend. Treat each other like friends as well.'

Things to do this week . . .

- Practise sharing the work that needs doing at home. Offer to help more. Work together as friends of Jesus.
- Make some food together with someone else in your family, make the table look beautiful with flowers and candles, and say Grace together before you eat it.
- Get into the habit of talking with Jesus each morning, before you eat, and before you go to sleep. Carry on doing that until you are at least 70 years old!
- Make a prayer corner near your bed.

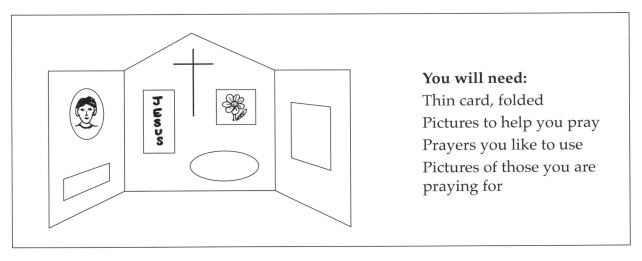

You will need:
Thin card, folded
Pictures to help you pray
Prayers you like to use
Pictures of those you are praying for

Week 5: Not servants but friends

Youth

This week's message for you from God . . .

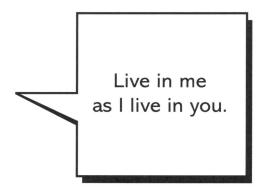

Live in me
as I live in you.

Jesus knew he wouldn't be walking around with an earthly body in quite the same way any more. He wanted his followers to know that even though they couldn't see him, he was fully alive and always there with them. So he talked about it as sharing his life. Jesus offers a friendship so close that we live in one another's life. That's quite an invitation. It's about talking everything over together, feeling comfortable in one another's company, working together like a team, looking out for one another's needs.

And this is a friendship for all the time we live in Time, as well as after death.

Things to do this week . . .

- Get into a habit of talking with Jesus every morning, every time you eat, and just before you go to sleep. Carry on till you're at least 70 years old!

- Practise living as a close friend of Jesus. You'll find yourself looking out for people's needs more and offering to help. You'll find yourself standing up for justice and speaking up for people who are oppressed. You'll find you're more confident to be yourself, and you'll be doing a bit of bridge-building, perhaps at school or at home. You'll want to put things right when they go wrong. Your life and Jesus' life together. What a team!

- Do something generous for someone you dislike or find difficult to cope with.

- Express this shared life in art, music or words.

Week 5: Not servants but friends

Adults

This week's message for you from God . . .

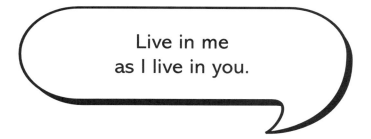

Live in me
as I live in you.

By the end of his time in the desert, Jesus was clearer than ever about his work on earth. The power and healing within him was to be used in a life of loving outreach, even though it would make him completely vulnerable. Jesus was to proclaim God's kingdom in signs and teaching, even though it would lead to rejection by the very humans he had come to save. Too costly? Jesus didn't think so. And it's this Jesus and this path that we are invited to follow as Christians.

Turning up on a Sunday to worship is important, but only one part of the total experience. We're invited to 'live in' Jesus as he 'lives in' us, and life, as our own lungs and heart show us, is a 24/7 programme. That means we can be assured of Jesus' presence at any time and all the time. But the friendship is two-way. We are invited to live in Jesus as well as he in us. Go for the total experience!

This week's assignment . . .

- Put prayer cards, small crosses or anything which reminds you of The Friendship all around your home and in the car, on your bag and so on, so that you keep getting reminded of it. This will help you build a relationship of 'praying constantly'.
- Choose a picture, prayer or Bible text which means a lot to you and bring that for the display this week.

All-age ideas for the Sundays in Lent

First Sunday in Lent, Years A, B and C

Focus of service: Temptation. Jesus in the desert.

Mood: Serious and self-aware. Attentive to what God is saying to us.

Possibilities for worship:
- Purple streamers and flags available during singing.
- Bowl of incense or fragrant oil burner burning during time of Penitence.
- In all three years the Old Testament reading can be dramatised or read chorally, with music background.
- Use two different voices for the conversation in the Gospel.
- Project image of the Judean desert and of large pebbles or boulders as a focus during time of Penitence and Gospel.
- Year B: Projected images of water and rainbow.
- Have a 'Hints for dealing with temptation' display during Lent where people of all ages can write (or have scribed) methods they have found useful in the battle of good over evil.

Prayer areas:
- Purple fabric.
- A few large smooth stones and some bread rolls all together.
- Two apples with bites taken out of them.
- Large question marks.
- Soundbites from the Gospel printed out separately among the images and prayer suggestions.
- Prayer suggestions: Pray for those battling with temptation at the moment; pray for all who lead and all who advise – for wisdom and integrity; pray for our wills to be lined up with God's will; pray for all who go hungry and thirsty; pray for those who have more than enough and refuse to share; pray for those who don't know what to do for the best.

Second Sunday of Lent, Years A, B and C

Focus of service: Living by faith in God.

Mood: Possibly disturbing – shaking us up. An honest look at the implications of the faith life. Challenging.

Possibilities for worship:

- Purple streamers and flags available for times of singing.
- At time of Penitence use your hands to make fists 'holding' the things you want God to forgive. Open up your hands as you tell God you are sorry. Hold them open to receive God's forgiveness.
- Use music as a background to the Old Testament reading as God speaks to Abraham.
- Have different voices in the Gospel conversations.
- Projected images of the desert again, and of the effects of a strong wind blowing (sailing boats, balloons, flags).
- Give space for people to be in silence waiting on God, using music to help reach the stillness, and a visual focus such as one of the windows, the cross or a projected painting such as Holman Hunt's 'The Light of the World'.

Prayer areas:

- Purple fabric or sand and rock arranged on plastic sheeting.
- Candles available to light.
- Pictures of contrasts in lifestyle and facilities available worldwide.
- Suggestions for prayer: Pray that we may wake up to what it means to live by faith in God; pray for those who find it very hard to trust God; pray for the grace to follow wherever God leads us; pray that we may not get in God's way or make it difficult for others to know him.
- Print out soundbites from the readings among the pictures.

Third Sunday in Lent, Years A, B and C

Focus of service: God's lavish and generous invitation to us, and the cost of responding with love and obedience.

Mood: Freeing, healing and also challenging.

Possibilities for worship:

- Green and blue streamers like water, or purple for the continuing Lenten colour.
- Recorded sounds of running water during the 'thirsty' Old Testament reading (Years A and C).
- Year A: Have the Gospel read in parts from the *Dramatised Bible* (or DIY).
- Year B: Act out the Gospel.
- Projected images of water, an ancient pathway or stone stairway.
- If the church has the Ten Commandments written up, focus on them during the time of Penitence, or use symbols for each of the commandments.
- Choose soundbites and write them large in bubble writing on lining paper with crayons available for colouring.
- Have the font open and full with a towel, so people can use it. Place the words 'Living God, satisfy our thirst' beside it.

Prayer areas:

- Use the font as one of the focus areas for prayer.
- Purple fabric or sand and stones with water.
- Have a jug of water and bowl.
- Pictures and information of fresh-water projects worldwide.
- A Bible open at the readings for today.
- Prayer suggestions: Pray for all who thirst for meaning in their lives; pray for those who have been baptised in this church; pray for courage to stand firm when the life of faith is challenging; pray for greater generosity of spirit.

Fourth Sunday of Lent (Mothering Sunday), Years A, B and C

Focus of service: Thanksgiving for earthly mothering of all kinds. Thanks for God's parenting of us.

Mood: Thankfulness and appreciation. Loving care and affirmation. Festive. Refreshing.

Possibilities for worship:

- Pink and purple streamers, strips of cloth hangings, banners or flags.
- Bells and shakers available.
- Projected images of mothering – people, animals and birds. Spring beauty in nature.
- Lots of flowers, both in arrangements and in small posies for giving to one another.
- Act out the Old Testament reading with music background.
- Short interview with different generations of mums and different generations of children.
- A 'God's Parenting' display on stands or projected: 'God is . . .'
- If using the second Gospel choice, focus on any places in the building which show Mary and John at the cross.
- Sounds of birdsong as people come in and during Communion.

Prayer areas:

- Pink and purple fabric with flowers among stones and 'mother and child' images from nature.
- Candles and quiet, refreshing music.
- One prayer focus for candles and flowers in memory of mothers who have died.
- Use the decorated font for a prayer focus of healing of damaged relationships.
- Suggestions for prayer: Thank God for all good mothering and all loving, caring relationships; pray for all families; give thanks for God's forgiveness and loving kindness; ask God to help us understand one another's needs better; we are all his children – ask him to help us grow in love.

Fifth Sunday of Lent, Years A, B and C

Focus of service: The way Jesus can transform suffering and death into life and hope.

Mood: Solemn. An engagement with the deep questions about life and death. Hope in the heart of suffering.

Possibilities for worship:

- Purple and hessian or unbleached cotton.
- Recorded music with an ache in it – such as *Schindler's List* or *Gladiator* – as a background to the Old Testament reading.
- Ongoing painting by one praying person during the worship, on a large scale (sheeting or lining paper), of the cross with a sense of glory as well as darkness.
- Projected images of dark thunderclouds with brightness, and of the bright day from inside the dark walls of a cave.
- Oil burner or bowl of incense to use during the Gospel.
- Shakers and wood blocks accompanying Ezekiel's dry bones vision.
- At the time of Penitence use Allegri's *Miserere* with the words 'Have mercy on me, O God' projected as they are carefully written.
- For the creed say the 'Glory to the Father, and to the Son . . .' and ask everyone to pause, catching their breath, immediately after 'is now . . .'.

Prayer areas:

- Have water available at the font with a towel, and images of the washing of feet.
- Use the whole building, drawing people to focus on any windows or architecture as symbols to direct their prayer. (There is often a variety of ways the Passion is portrayed.)
- Purple fabric, rocks, thorns, a cross.
- Suggestions for prayer: Pray for those who are grieving; pray for a deeper awareness of living eternal life here and now; pray for courage for those going through times of darkness and shadow; pray for a clearer and more honest understanding of who we are; pray for a cleansing of all motives.
- Have headlines and news pictures placed among the prayer intentions with post-its and pens available to write prayers on.

Palm Sunday, Years A, B and C

Focus of service: Jesus entering Jerusalem on a donkey. The Servant King facing rejection and death to free us from everlasting death.

Mood: Bitter/sweet. Rejoicing and yet heavy with the shadow of the cross. Fresh awareness of our own human fickleness.

Possibilities for worship:

- Purple hangings. Plain cross draped with cloth, the base in among stones.
- Symbols of Jesus' death brought to the cross during the offertory – nails, hammer, dice, rope, coins thrown down from a bag, thorns, a tall reed.
- Palm branches, any branches, streamers and flags for the procession, preferably outside. Songs that everyone can sing at a pitch they can reach, during the procession. Even a donkey, perhaps?
- Dramatised choral reading of the long Gospel; involve the whole gathered people. Or try a recorded version.
- Where there are Stations of the Cross, walk in procession around these as the story is narrated. Or make a 'Way of the Cross' outside and all around the church with the Gospel read as everyone walks it together.
- At some point in the worship, encourage everyone who can to kneel, even if this isn't usual practice.
- For the time of Penitence, place on the floor a cross of lit candles in sand.
- Projected images of the Crucifixion through art.

Prayer areas:

- Stones and thorns, with soundbites from the Gospel narrative printed among them.
- Focus on the crosses around the building.
- Provide tiny crosses to hold and place in the prayer areas.
- Different images of Christ projected or displayed.
- Suggestions for prayer: Pray for the world to want God's kingdom; pray for God's peace which the world cannot give; pray for those imprisoned who are innocent; pray for better discernment to recognise propaganda for what it is and hold firm to the truth.

All-age ideas for Holy Week

Maundy Thursday

Focus of service: The Last Supper. The Passover with new meaning of Bread and Wine. Servanthood and foot-washing. The command to love one another as Jesus loves us.

Mood: Solemn and important for the whole community. Reflective and thankful. Mystical.

Possibilities for worship:
- Consider a Eucharist in the context of a Passover celebration (see page 66).
- White and gold cloth, streamers and flags.
- Projected images of foot-washing, bread and wine, wheat and grapes.
- Bread and wine with wheat and grapes in a focal display.
- Foot-washing – with several bowls and towels so everyone can wash one another's feet.
- Set up a 'Garden of Gethsemane' with plants, rocks and water, and hold a prayer vigil through the night.

Good Friday

Focus of the service: The Crucifixion. Jesus loving us even to death. Love that saves us and sets us free.

Mood: Solemn. Sad. Penitential. Thankful. Touching the raw places of our deepest reality. Love for Jesus.

Possibilities for worship:
- Have the church building open for prayer, with focuses which introduce people to Jesus and the extent of God's forgiving love for us all (see pages 43, 50).
- Join with Christians from other churches for a combined walk and service using readings from the Gospel, prayers and music (see page 53).
- Collect a whole range of images of the crucifixion and of Christ from art, and encourage people to wander around them, choosing one that draws them, while music is playing.
- Make a prayer trail of the Way of the Cross around the church grounds or a local beauty spot, and have copies like a nature trail so visitors can follow it on their own or in small groups (see page 60).

'Open church' days in Lent

Many people have a strong faith in God but find the whole idea of attending a church service in the traditional way very alien. On the other hand, people of all ages and cultures will often appreciate the opportunity to wander around an open church, or spend time quietly in God's presence there.

If this is what so many find helpful in deepening a relationship with God, it is surely important that we hear the requests for churches to be open and provide times when, rather than a service, the space is simply available and welcoming as God's house – houses of prayer.

There are many ways we can give sensitive guidance without taking control over the way people spend their time in church. So often the very buildings speak eloquently without our having to do anything except join the praying, kneeling quietly and reverently, making ourselves still and attentive, or walking around the church, praying as we go.

This simple, regular habit of praying in churches has got lost somewhere under a pile of insurance regulations and an imbalance between doing and being, and it is a loss which saps the whole church of life and energy. It's well worth starting from the gap and building up a fresh understanding of those extraordinary buildings of ours – as places where anyone can go, regularly or occasionally, to meet with the living God.

Here are some ideas for ways in which to help visitors and regular worshippers alike, of all ages, into the Godly conversation we know as prayer. There is a seasonal flavour here, so that everyone can be following the Lent journey together.

Design a desert

You will need a plastic sandpit. Fill it with sand and some big stones. Provide a box in which there are model palm trees and bushes, some wild animals, such as a lion, a few goats, wolves or jackals, and camels. Have a small metal mirror which can be used as a water hole. You will also need a model of Jesus.

Print, photocopy or write out the instructions on the following page and display attractively:

Design a desert

(Younger children need to work with an older child or an adult.)

- **Make this into a desert with hills and valleys.**

- **Where will any water collect? Make the mirror a water pool.**

- **Where might the animals be in the daytime? And in the night time? You can move them around.**

- **Jesus spent 40 days in the desert on his own before he started his work of showing everyone what it's like to live in God's kingdom. Make Jesus wander about in the desert you have made.**

- **He had nothing to eat and he was on his own. How do you think he felt?**

- **Why is Jesus out here in the desert? Read the account in the books of Matthew (chapter 4:1-11), Mark (chapter 1:9-13) or Luke (chapter 4:1-13) and think about it.**

- **Provide cut-out thought bubbles so you can jot down any ideas you have. See how your ideas compare with other people's thoughts.**

Stage a play

This can also take place at the desert landscape, or alternatively use two simple hand puppets against a desert backdrop painted on flipchart paper or on a display board. You need to prepare the script written out on coloured card and strung together like this:

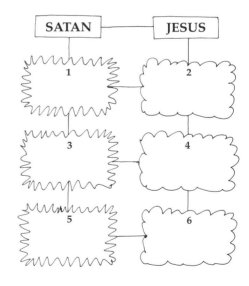

1. Use your power to make these stones into bread, if you're the Son of God.
2. You don't only need bread to keep alive – you need God's words too.
3. Jump down and show them you're superhuman, if you're the Son of God.
4. Don't try to test your God.
5. I'll give you all these kingdoms if you bow down and worship me.
6. Go away, Satan! The scripture says, 'You shall worship God and serve only him.'

Once again, write or print out the instructions clearly and display them attractively:

Stage a play

- Find a partner to act with.

- One of you is Jesus and the other is Satan – the devil.

- Satan reads the red, jagged cards, and Jesus reads the red thought-bubble cards. Read the numbers in the right order.

- The person who is Jesus moves the model Jesus around in the desert. Choose together where Jesus might be for each of the three conversations.

Learn how to deal with temptation

This is something which people often appreciate help with, but the church is oddly shy about offering practical help based on scripture. Lent open-church days provide opportunities to address it.

Prepare a focus with draped purple fabric, a few large stones, and a candle burning surrounded by barbed wire. On different pieces of card, print or write out in full the following verses, using a translation of your choice, most appropriate to your situation.

Psalm 3:3, 6:8, 51:7, 51:11, 95:7, 146:7; Jeremiah 9:23, 24; Micah 6:8; Matthew 6:24, 7:12; Mark 6:50-51, 8:34-36; Luke 6:37-38, 6:47-48, 12:29-32, 22:46; John 6:27, 10:9-10, 14:27; 1 John 3:11.

Scatter these cards so that people can skim-read them and choose one to work with. Have some blank cards available too. And here are the instructions, to be copied and displayed:

Be prepared! Watch and pray!

- Satan is always tempting us all to choose what is bad for us or bad for others or bad for our world. Jesus warned his followers, 'Watch and pray so you don't fall in with temptation.'

- Notice how Jesus fights the temptations. He quotes words from the Bible which he already knows really well. We can arm ourselves in the same way.

- Choose a card, find somewhere quiet in church to sit, or walk around learning it by heart. When you have learnt it, write it out on one of the blank cards from memory, and take it home with you. Pass it on to someone else.

Jesus, wash my sin away

Fill the font with water and have a jug of water available, and water to drink. At the edge of the water have these words written: 'Go in peace; the Lord has put away your sin.' Nearby provide towels, a Bible, and a picture of John baptising in the River Jordan. Make sure appropriate people are available. Display the following instructions clearly.

Jesus, wash my sin away

- Does your sin haunt you? Would you love to be free of it? Would you like Jesus to forgive you and wash it away for ever?

- Then this is what to do. Name the sin in you that shuts you off from God and is imprisoning you. Tell God about it, remembering those it may have hurt, and tell him you are sorry and want to repent – or turn your back on sin. Ask God to forgive you and wash you clean. (You can do this work with God through a priest, or minister, or on your own, whichever you find most helpful.)

- God forgives everyone who turns to him and repents. Nothing at all is too evil for him to forgive.

- Use the water in the font to wash your hands in as a sign of your longing to be washed clean of sin. You might like to drink some water as well.

- As you wash, read the words of God's forgiveness. They are true and you can trust them.

- Find a quiet place in church to thank God for his mercy and love.

'Look, here is the Lamb of God who takes away the sin of the world!'

The sanctuary, or the area around the holy table, can be used to focus on the words of John the Baptist when he had seen the Spirit descending on Jesus at his baptism.

The meaning and power of this metaphor is lost on us unless we understand where it's coming from, and how those listening to John the Baptist would have understood it. This is a good opportunity to find out what John the Baptist was getting at.

- Display a toy lamb with an illustrated Bible open at an appropriate picture of the story, and the following explanation beside it:

> It was the Passover lamb which had saved
> the people of Israel from the plague of death,
> and opened the way for them to escape
> to freedom from slavery in Egypt.

- Display a Bible open at Isaiah 53:4-7, or write out these verses with some letters illuminated, and pens for colouring available. Place beside it the following explanation:

John the Baptist was a prophet. He could see that Jesus was God's 'lamb'.

It was Jesus who would save people from the plague of evil and open the way for them to escape from being enslaved by sin to the freedom of full life, through being forgiven.

And it wouldn't just be the people of Israel, but everyone, in every country and in every generation.

Like an innocent lamb being offered for sacrifice, Jesus, without sin, would willingly give his life so that we could be healed.

Wonderful news!

Near a window provide a number of mirrors – full length down to pocket size. Arrange them so people can see themselves from different angles. Print, decorate and display the words of the Beatitudes, from Tom Wright's version in *Matthew for Everyone**. Significantly, he translates 'Blessed' as 'Wonderful news' – a reminder that this passage is about God's good news being announced.

---

* Tom Wright, *Matthew for Everyone, Part 1* (SPCK, 2002) pages 34-35.

The Beatitudes

Wonderful news for the poor in spirit! The kingdom of heaven is yours.
Wonderful news for the mourners! You're going to be comforted.
Wonderful news for the meek! You're going to inherit the earth.
Wonderful news for those who hunger and thirst for God's justice!
    You're going to be satisfied.
Wonderful news for the merciful! You'll receive mercy yourselves.
Wonderful news for the pure in heart! You will see God.
Wonderful news for the peacemakers! You'll be called God's children.
Wonderful news for people who are persecuted because of God's way!
    The kingdom of heaven belongs to you.
Wonderful news for you, when people slander you and persecute you,
    and say all kinds of wicked things about you falsely because of me!
Celebrate and rejoice: there's a great reward for you in heaven. That's how
    they persecuted the prophets who went before you.

• Print out this poem as well:

In the space
between the mirror and my face
Hope becomes Reality.
The world is reversed
in the light of God's strangeness
and the strange becomes safe.
What will I see in the reflection?
Potential for God's grace.
And in that,
freedom.

Rachel Summers

• Print out and display the instructions:

God's wonderful news

- **Notice how the mirror turns things round. (God's values – which set us free to live life to the full – are a reverse image of worldly values which enslave us.)**

- **Look in the mirror and see yourself as God sees you. (God looks on the heart, not outward appearance.) God thinks you are beautiful, and he loves you.**

- **Now read the poem. God has all the grace you need. It's there for the asking. He intends you to live life to the full.**

- **Look at how the light shines through the windows. Let God's kingdom life shine through you, warming you and filling you with light.**

The church library

Make an attractive area with rugs and places to sit, with areas for adults and children. Borrow the books from the local library and from willing lenders, with 'menu cards' giving titles and page numbers for the appropriate extracts. Have people available to read with any who find reading difficult.

At all levels we are exploring the way we find out who we really are, and how God has given us the freedom to choose how we live.

Here are some ideas for the different age groups.

- **Young children**: Picture books of children playing, making things, eating, sleeping and so on. Interactive books which let the child choose and make things happen. Books like *Elmer the Elephant, The Lion who Wanted to Love*, and *Dogger*.

- **Older children**: *The Silver Chair* (the part where the children are lost in the huge letters and suddenly realise they are right in the middle of the clue they need). *Harry Potter and the Chamber of Secrets* (the mirror of ERISED / DESIRE which shows you what you most long for, and Dumbledore's warning about wasting your life by sitting in front of it instead of really living.) *The Bed and Breakfast Star* (where being yourself turns out to be far more satisfying than all the pretending).

- **Youth**: Video loop and / or extract of *Lord of the Rings* (where the temptation of putting the ring on is really strong, and is fought against). Video loop of *The Matrix* (the choice of the blue or red pill). *Shadowmancer*, G. P. Taylor (where in a presence of holiness Thomas makes his life-changing choice – chapter 5).

- **Adults**: *About a Boy* (where Will is learning from Marcus how to tell the truth instead of pretending). *Matthew for Everyone, Part 1*, pages 34-38 (God's invitation to live in the kingdom straightaway). *The Puzzle of Evil*, chapter 15 (The challenge of freedom), pages 196-200.

Take up your cross and follow me

At regular times throughout the open church day have someone dressed in a white alb carrying a processional cross around the church – perhaps in a figure of eight (down south aisle, up centre, down north aisle and up centre), finishing at the front of the church. People are invited to walk along behind the cross, as a sign of their commitment to following Jesus in their lives. As the procession starts, someone reads Matthew 16:24-26, Mark 8:34-36 or Luke 9:23-25. Then everyone joins in the following prayer:

Lord Jesus,
I want to follow you
all the days of my life.
Amen.

The walk around the church can be made in silence (while all the other activities are going on), or a hymn can be sung, such as 'O Jesus, I have promised', 'He who would valiant be', 'I, the Lord of sea and sky', 'Take up your cross, he says', 'Step by step' or 'I'm coming back to the heart of worship'.

When the procession reaches the altar, everyone joins in the Lord's Prayer, and people are invited to make a cross from small sticks and bag fastening wire, to take away with them as a reminder of the commitment they have made.

Kite-making

'The wind blows where it chooses, and you hear the sound of it,
but you do not know where it comes from or where it goes.
So it is with everyone born of the Spirit.'

DANGER ALERT

NEVER fly kites in storms
or near trees, electricity pylons,
airports or busy roads!

Lent is often quite a windy time of year – a good time for making a kite and flying it. Kite-flying is also a reminder, or symbol, of the way we need to be flexible enough to move in the powerful breath of God's Spirit, but also anchored and firmly rooted in the power of God's love.

These kites can be made quite easily if the more skilled help the less skilled. The basic shape makes for a very stable flyer, and, of course, the decorations can be as varied and imaginative as you like. You might open up a kite-making session to the local neighbourhood, or give out patterns and instructions for households and friendship groups to make their models and bring them to an open space for a flying session. You could stick to the Lent colours of purple and sackcloth, or use the rainbow of God's promise as your inspiration. Write a message on the kite's tail – here are some suggestions:

- God created the heavens and the earth.
- Heaven and earth are full of your glory!
- Jesus is Lord!
- Glory to God in the highest!
- Remember, I am with you always!
- Breathe on us, breath of God!

Cut several templates of the basic shape so everyone can mark it out on a plastic bin bag, closely woven fabric, or from a length of thick plastic sheeting. Decorate using stickers, freezer labels cut in shapes, oil or acrylic paints, or powder paints mixed with PVA glue. Kite string can be bought at craft shops, or you can use button thread from a furniture upholstery shop. Curtain rings can be bought at a DIY shop or Woolworth's. Wind the kite-string round a thick cardboard tube, securing on the first wind with a strong knot, so your kite doesn't escape accidentally.

So long as you get the proportions right, you can make this kite any size from small to enormous. As a general rule, the smaller the person flying the kite, the smaller the kite needs to be. Otherwise kite-flying can be too much of a challenge to young children, and they end up doing nothing while someone bigger gets all the fun. Little kites work nicely even when you just run around in the wind.

Here are the instructions:

How to make a kite

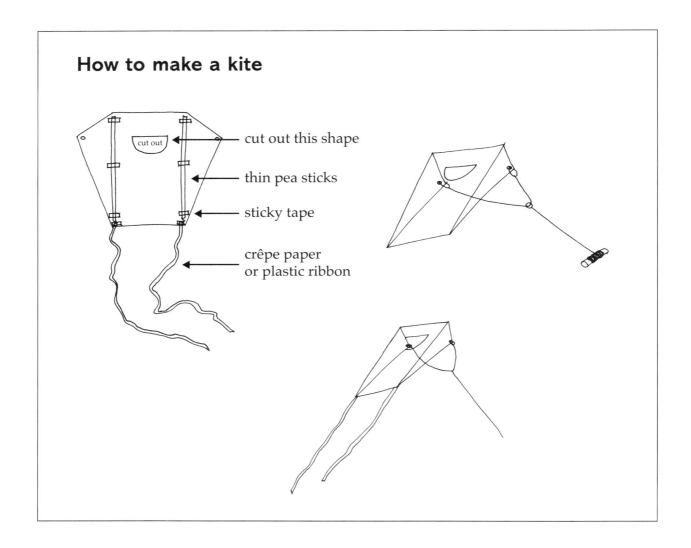

cut out this shape

thin pea sticks

sticky tape

crêpe paper
or plastic ribbon

How to fly a kite

Remember: higher means windier and kites need wind to fly.

1. Roll up the string close to the kite. Stand with the wind right behind you.
2. Let out a few metres of line. A friend can now lift your kite into the sky as you coax it higher by pulling on the line or walking backwards. Or you can lift it yourself and walk quickly backwards to make the line taut (tight).
3. Let out more line so the kite can climb upwards.
4. Pulling on the line helps balance the kite whenever the wind drops a bit.

Holy walking

'I am the Way . . .'

After his baptism Jesus went off into his local desert, and during his ministry he would often walk into the hills to pray. There is a long tradition of pilgrimage and the value of holy journeying, either alone or in community with others, so that the physical journey focuses our attention on our spiritual journey through life.

Lent is a good time for a church pilgrimage of some kind. There are plenty to choose from, as pilgrimages have become quite popular again. Both journey and destination are of importance in a pilgrimage, and there may well be a traditionally 'holy place' not far from your area. If so, consider a day out to it. Travelling together, whether in shared cars, a coach or on public transport, is all part of the experience.

If you are too far from a traditional 'holy place', don't worry, because in a sense everywhere is holy, being part of God's marvellous creation! Just choose a beautiful place and go there.

A picnic or shared lunch will probably need to be indoors somewhere at this time of year, but there are all kinds of possibilities for this, such as family rooms in pubs, community centres and local churches. Include at least part of the day as a walk, manageable for all ages, and wheelchair/pushchair friendly.

Have one or two people to check out the possibilities in person beforehand, so that you can provide everyone with a simple map of the route for the walk, with prayers and Bible references and things to notice along the way, like a nature trail. If there is a suitable open space, take kites with you (see page 52) and have a kite-flying session.

Here are some suggestions for worship you may like to include in your church's holy walk:

As you set out from the church

Lord Jesus,
you often walked up into the hills to pray,
and we are setting off now
to spend today in your company.
Guide our steps, and lead us into a closer friendship with you.
Teach us the way of love, looking out for one another's needs.
Teach us to notice the wonder of creation.
Keep us thankful and keep us safe.
Amen.

As you begin the walk

Who is the One we worship?
We worship the One True God, Father, Son and Holy Spirit.
What are we seeking on this walk together?
To walk with Jesus, who is the Way, the Truth and the Life.
Let us walk in the love and peace of Christ.
Thanks be to God.

As you walk together you may like to sing, chat, and have a short time of walking in silence as you get close to your destination.

Some prayers for the stopping places

With the good sky above us
and the good earth beneath our feet,
we give our thanks and praise to God
who has made all things well.
Amen.

As the earth is open to receive sunlight and rain,
light and darkness,
so make us ready to receive from you, O God,
and be thankful.
Amen.

As we discover more about you, O Lord,
so we discover more about ourselves.
Give us grace to become the people
you have called us to be.
Amen.

Before you eat

Use one of the prayers on page 11 or one of these:

All good gifts around us
are sent from heaven above;
then thank the Lord, O thank the Lord,
for all his love.

As we eat together
in God's company,
so may we grow together
in God's love.
Amen.

Include a short time of worship at the heart of the holy place. The style of this will vary according to the kind of place and the tradition of worship in your church, of course, but take care to make it accessible for all age groups, using the senses, and keeping it short. The important thing is to give people the opportunity of catching a sense of God's presence in this place.

Start with some sung praise and worship, include one of the following readings from scripture, have a time of sharing anything people have noticed on the walk, pray together and sing something lively and uplifting to finish.

Possible readings:
- Exodus 3:1-6 (Moses meets with God at Horeb, the holy mountain)
- 1 Kings 19:8-13 (Elijah meets with God at Horeb, the holy mountain)
- Matthew 17:1-8 (the disciples see Jesus transfigured on the mountain)

When you return home

O give thanks to the Lord for he is good;
his love lasts for ever. Alleluia!

Growing in holiness together

'Some seed fell in good soil . . .'

An Easter garden can be the result of a 'growing' programme throughout Lent for the whole church community. This is how it works. Everyone takes on the challenge of growing something for the church Easter garden, and the daily care of the plants is linked with daily prayer and Bible reading. On Holy Saturday – the Saturday before Easter Sunday – all the plants are assembled, like one of those flower show gardens, so that Easter has grown organically and spiritually out of our shared Lenten commitment.

Some things can be grown from seed, such as grass and herbs. Others will need to be started as bulbs and seedlings and grown on during Lent to flowering. Start feeding the information about the growing project a few weeks before Lent begins, so that people are prepared for it. Ask a few gardeners for advice about what best to grow in your area, and if anyone can start the seedlings off at home, that will save money and keep the project as home-grown as possible. But work closely with a local garden centre, so as to draw them into the project. They may even be prepared to offer you space on their premises to create a second garden – a lovely opportunity for outreach and inclusion.

Give out the seeds and seedlings on Shrove Tuesday or Ash Wednesday, or the first Sunday of Lent, together with growing instructions and the accompanying prayer and Bible reading (see below). Throughout Lent keep a progress report going on the weekly handout to encourage people, and you may like to construct a section of the garden each week, either inside the church or outside if this is more appropriate.

Week 1: the heavy plastic sheeting

Week 2: rocks around the edges

Week 3: the soil

Week 4: the cave tomb and stony path

Week 5: the crosses on the hill

Holy Week: assemble the garden with all the plants

This is the daily prayer and Bible reading programme to be given out to everyone:

Growing together *

Jesus explained lots of things to the people in stories. 'Listen to this!' he'd say. 'Don't let it go in one ear and out of the other – really listen to it so you hear with your heart as well as your ears!' And this is one of the stories he told.

A farmer went out sowing seed. As he was scattering the seeds, some fell on the path, and the birds swooped down and ate them, so they didn't grow at

---

* A photocopiable version to make a four-page A5 leaflet can be found on page 88.

all. Some of the seeds fell where the ground was rocky, so the young shoots grew fast all right, but they wilted and died away as soon as the strong sun burnt down on them. That's because they hadn't had room to grow a strong root system in the shallow earth. Some other seeds fell in the middle of where the thorns and weeds were growing. Weeds grow faster and stronger than wheat, and they choked the young shoots so they died away. But other seeds fell in the right place, in the good, rich earth prepared for them, so that they grew up strong and tall, and yielded a good crop – 100 per cent, 60 per cent or 30 per cent increase on what had been sown.
Based on Matthew 13:3-9

This Lent we are all going to grow a plant, taking care of it and watering it. Then we'll bring the plants to church in the week before Easter, and they will all become part of a special Easter garden. Keep the A5 leaflet next to your plant and read it every day.

A daily growing prayer

Lord Jesus,
may your kingdom grow in us
and may your will be done.
Amen.

Forty daily readings from the Psalms
to help the kingdom grow in you

1. You show me the path of life. In your presence there is fullness of joy. *Psalm 16:11*

2. It is you who light my lamp; the Lord my God lights up my darkness. *Psalm 18:28*

3. The Lord is my shepherd; there is nothing else I need. *Psalm 23:1*

4. To you, O Lord, I lift up my soul. O my God, in you I trust. *Psalm 25:1, 2*

5. Make me to know your ways, O Lord; teach me your paths. *Psalm 25:4*

6. All the paths of the Lord are steadfast love and faithfulness. *Psalm 25:10*

7. Keep your tongue from evil and your lips from speaking lies. Depart from evil and do good. Psalm *34:13, 14*

8. Be still before the Lord and wait patiently for him. *Psalm 37:7*

9. Depart from evil and do good; so you shall abide for ever. For the Lord loves justice; he will not forsake his faithful ones. *Psalm 37:27, 28*

10. I waited patiently for the Lord; he leaned over to me and heard my cry. He drew me up from the desolate pit, out of the muddy swamp, and set my feet upon a rock, making my steps secure. *Psalm 40:1, 2*

11. As the deer longs for flowing streams, so my soul longs for you, O God. My soul thirsts for God, for the living God. *Psalm 42:1*

12. Why are you cast down, O my soul, and why are you disquieted within me? Hope in God; for I shall again praise him, my help and my God. Psalm *42:11*

13. Be still and know that I am God! *Psalm 46:10*

14. For you have been my help, and in the shadow of your wings I sing for joy. *Psalm 63:7*

15. Glorious are you, more majestic than the everlasting mountains. *Psalm 76:4*

16. I cry aloud to God that he may hear me. In the day of my trouble I seek the Lord. *Psalm 77:1, 2*

17. Things that we have heard and known, that our ancestors have told us, we will not hide them from their children; we will tell to the coming generation the glorious deeds of the Lord . . . and the wonders he has done. *Psalm 78:3, 4*

18. Happy is everyone who trusts in you. *Psalm 84:12*

19. For you, O Lord, are good and forgiving. *Psalm 86:5*

20. You are merciful and gracious, slow to anger and of great faithfulness. *Psalm 86:15*

21. The heavens are yours, the earth also is yours; the world and all that is in it – you have created them. *Psalm 89:11*

22. Before the mountains were born, before you had formed the earth and the world, from everlasting to everlasting you are God. *Psalm 90:2*

23. For a thousand years in your sight are like yesterday when it is past . . . *Psalm 90:4*

24. O come, let us worship and bow down, let us kneel before the Lord our Maker! For he is our God and we are the people of his pasture, and the sheep of his hand. *Psalm 95:6, 7*

25. Bless the Lord, O my soul, and all that is within me, bless his holy name. *Psalm 103:1*

26. He turns a desert into pools of water, a parched land into springs of water. *Psalm 107:35*

27. He raises the poor from the dust, and lifts the needy from the ash heap. *Psalm 113:7*

28. Out of my distress I called on the Lord; he answered me and set me in a broad place. With the Lord at my side I do not fear. *Psalm 118:5, 6*

29. I treasure your word in my heart, so that I may not sin against you. *Psalm 119:11*

30. The Lord is your keeper; the Lord is your shade at your right hand. The sun shall not strike you by day, nor the moon by night. *Psalm 121:5, 6*

31. With the Lord there is steadfast love, and with him is great power to redeem. *Psalm 130:7*

32. O Lord, you have searched me and known me, you know when I sit down and when I rise up . . . you search out my path and my lying down, and are familiar with all my ways. *Psalm 139:1-3*

33. Set a guard over my mouth, O Lord; keep watch over the door of my lips. *Psalm 141:3*

34. My eyes are turned towards you, O God, my Lord; in you I seek refuge. *Psalm 141:8*

35. Let me hear of your steadfast love in the morning, for in you I put my trust. Teach me the way I should go, for to you I lift up my soul. *Psalm 143:8*

36. The Lord is gracious and merciful, slow to anger and abounding in steadfast love. The Lord is good to all, and his compassion is over all that he has made. *Psalm 145:8, 9*

37. The Lord is just in all his ways, and kind in all his doings. The Lord is near to all who call on him, to all who call on him in truth. *Psalm 145:17, 18*

38. The Lord sets the prisoners free; the Lord opens the eyes of the blind. The Lord lifts up those who are bowed down. *Psalm 146:8*

39. The Lord heals the broken-hearted and binds up their wounds. *Psalm 147:3*

40. Praise him, sun and moon; praise him all you shining stars! Let them praise the Lord for he commanded and they were created. *Psalm 148:3, 5*

Let everything that has breath praise the Lord! Alleluia! *Psalm 150:6*

Making a prayer trail

'Lord, teach us to pray.'

Some churches have around their walls the Stations of the Cross. Originally these were introduced to local churches so that those who were unable to make a pilgrimage to Jerusalem could still experience the Via Dolorosa, following in the footsteps of Jesus as he walked and stumbled, carrying the weight of the crosspiece through the city streets and out to the place of his execution. All along that route in Jerusalem (or at least the likely route for it) there are places to stop and pray, reflecting on the enormity of that journey and its significance for the whole human race.

Whether or not your church has the traditional 'Stations' or stopping places of prayer, the idea of a prayer trail like this is such a good one that it can easily be adapted and refreshed to work across the denominations and for all traditions. And because it is practical and multi-sensory, with differentiation largely through outcome and response, it is suitable for all age groups. The young children search for the next number and look at the picture at each station while the older members of the community say the words. Everyone can join in the repeated response. Sing a chorus or verse of a hymn while moving from one station to the next.

Think of it a bit like a nature trail. At the most basic, you will need numbered places around the church and its grounds, together with a simple map on the leaflet which people can follow, either alone or in groups. Or you can have people dressed up in a tableau at each station. Site the places of prayer so that they enrich or help the prayer focus. For instance, choose a place near nettles and thorns, or recycling bins, for Trail B, station 5; a place near the altar table, or near a baker's for Trail A, station 6; the font or a river or pond for Trail A, station 9. Use features you have in the church or your local town which portray any of the events, and display prints of works of art, home-made art from representatives of all age groups, or a real-life tableau at each place of prayer. Children can collect a sticker from each station as they visit it on the trail.

Prayer trail A: 'Follow me!'

Station 1
Jesus is born as a baby

- God made the whole universe, and now here is God, coming to live among us in person as a little baby! Let that sink in, and then say thank you to God in your own words.
- Read John 1:14: 'And the Word became flesh and dwelt among us, and we have seen his glory, the glory as of the Father's Son, full of grace and truth.' *or*

  Luke 2:7: 'And she gave birth to her firstborn son and wrapped him in bands of cloth, and laid him in a manger, because there was no room for him in the inn.'
- Will you follow Jesus in the way of littleness?
  With the help of God, I will.

Station 2
Jesus grows up to be a carpenter

- As Jesus grew up he watched and helped Joseph making things from wood. He watched and helped Mary making bread. Jesus grew up on the same planet we live on. He would have laughed and cried and told jokes and been upset, just like the rest of us. Jesus knows what it's like to be human. Talk over with Jesus your fears and hopes.
- Read Luke 3:23: 'Jesus was about thirty years old when he began his work.'
- Will you follow Jesus in the ordinary, everyday things of life?
  With the help of God, I will.

Station 3
Jesus proclaims the kingdom of God

- People had long been waiting for God's kingdom to come, with God's Christ coming to live among them in person. Jesus showed them, with signs of healing and words full of God's loving forgiveness, that the kingdom was here at last. God was with his people in person. Imagine yourself being there at one of the healings, or when the 5000 people were fed. Pray for anyone who is hurting, or who doesn't know Jesus yet.
- Read Luke 9:11: 'Jesus welcomed the crowds and spoke to them about the kingdom of God, and healed those who needed to be cured.'
- Will you follow Jesus, ready to speak with people about the kingdom?
  With the help of God I will.

Station 4
Jesus calls his disciples to follow him

- Jesus chose and called twelve people as his disciples, or students. He taught them about living God's way. They walked with him every day and saw the way he lived and prayed. They asked him questions and listened to the answers he gave. He is calling you, now, to spend your life in his company.

- Read Luke 9:23: 'Then he said to them all, "If any want to become my followers, let them deny themselves and take up their cross daily and follow me. For those who want to save their life will lose it, and those who lose their life for my sake will save it."'

- Will you follow Jesus, even when it gets difficult?
  With the help of God, I will.

Station 5
Jesus rides into Jerusalem on a donkey

- A king would ride a grand horse, but Jesus came into the city on a donkey. The crowds welcomed him as their King and Saviour. Jesus was showing them that the kingdom wasn't what they had been expecting. It was a kingdom of love, not worldly power. Pray for the world leaders, and for God's kingdom of peace and love.

- Read Mark 10:42-44: 'You know that among the unbelievers those whom they recognise as rulers lord it over them . . . but it is not to be so among you; but whoever wishes to become great among you must be your servant . . . for the Son of Man came not to be served but to serve.'

- Will you follow Jesus by serving others with respect, however they treat you?
  With the help of God, I will.

Station 6
Jesus says, 'Do this . . .' at the Last Supper

- Jesus knew he was going to die for us. His life was being broken so we could be fed and live for ever in the dimension of heaven. He promised his friends that whenever they broke bread together remembering Jesus, then Jesus would be there in person and feed them all with his life. Pray for those in your own church.

- Read Luke 22:19: 'Then he took a loaf of bread, and when he had given thanks, he broke it, and gave it to them, saying, "This is my body, which is given for you. Do this in remembrance of me."'

- Will you follow Jesus, the Bread of Life?
  With the help of God, I will.

Station 7
Jesus is arrested

- Jesus was betrayed by one of his closest followers. Perhaps Judas gave up on Jesus because he wasn't the kind of Saviour Judas wanted. Jesus didn't use his power to escape. The way of love meant being there for us right through the darkest, loneliest times. Imagine how Jesus felt being arrested for being honest.

- Read John 15:12: 'This is my commandment, that you love one another as I have loved you.'

- Will you follow Jesus even when people insult you and falsely accuse you? **With the help of God, I will.**

Station 8
Jesus is crucified to death

- Jesus was given his own cross to carry to the place where he would be put to death. They put a sign up to say he was a king. And that was true in a way they didn't understand. His disciples ran away. The crowds laughed and jeered at him. Jesus prayed, 'Father, forgive them – they don't know what they're doing.' Pray for anyone you find it hard to forgive.

- Read Mark 15:39: 'Now when the centurion, who stood facing him, saw that in this way he breathed his last, he said, "Truly this man was God's Son!"'

- Will you follow Jesus wherever he leads you to go? **With the help of God, I will.**

Station 9
Jesus is alive again for ever

- Jesus' dead body was laid in a new tomb sealed with a stone and guarded by soldiers. Yet, early on the first day of the week, the stone had been rolled away and the tomb was empty. Jesus was alive with a new kind of life. He met people and talked and ate with them. He has been alive ever since that Sunday morning. Jesus is here with you now. Not dead, not a memory, but fully alive.

- Read Matthew 28:18-20: 'Jesus came and said to them, "All authority in heaven and earth has been given to me. Go therefore and make disciples of all nations, baptising them in the name of the Father and of the Son and of the Holy Spirit, and teaching them to obey everything that I have commanded you. And remember, I am with you always, to the end of the age."'

- Will you follow the Lord Jesus? **With the help of God I will.**

Invite everyone to join in praying the Lord's Prayer, in whatever form or language helps them most.

Finish with a Blessing.

Why not share some hot cross buns?

Prayer trail B: 'Lord, teach us to pray'

Station 1 (preferably outside)
Our Father in heaven, hallowed be your name

- What can you hear? What can you see? You are standing on the surface of a planet moving through space. The whole of creation is God's good idea. And yet we are invited to talk to him as a baby talks to the daddy she loves and trusts.

- Hold your thumb – the very human digit which enables us to make things – while you say the words: 'Our Father in heaven, hallowed be your name!'

Station 2 (stained glass of God as king)
Your kingdom come, your will be done on earth as in heaven

- The best that can happen for anyone, and in any situation, is for God's will to be done. You can't ask for anything better than for God's kingdom of love and peace to grow on earth.

- Hold your index finger – the authority finger – as you say the words: 'Your kingdom come, your will be done on earth as in heaven.'

Station 3 (picture of people who are hungry)
Give us today our daily bread

- God can only fulfil our needs if we have our hands and lives open to receive from him. And what we need is not always the same as what we want!

- Hold your middle finger and use it to open up your hand into the asking position as you say the words: 'Give us today our daily bread.'

Station 4 (a cross or crucifix)
And forgive us our sins as we forgive those who sin against us

- There are bound to be times when we have conflicts and upset each other. Part of loving is learning to say sorry to one another, and make up after a row. Life is too short to waste being bitter and angry.

- Hold your ring finger – the close relationships finger – as you say the words: 'And forgive us our sins as we forgive those who sin against us.'

Station 5 (dustbins, or thorns and nettles)
Lead us not into temptation but deliver us from evil

- Jesus warns us to watch and pray, so that we don't fall into temptation. We often forget to arm ourselves against sin and evil, but we do need to.

- Hold your weak little finger to remind you of your need to pray for strength as you say the words: 'Lead us not into temptation but deliver us from evil.'

Station 6 (an arrangement of flowers or a dramatic window)
For the kingdom, the power and the glory are yours, now and for ever

- This is an extra prayer of praise which is often added on to the five-finger way Jesus taught his disciples to pray. It takes us back to praising God, the Lord of all.

- Think again of the vast universe created by God and the way we are stuck on to the surface of one small planet by gravity, as you say the words: 'For the kingdom, the power and the glory are yours, now and for ever. Amen.'

A Passover celebration

'Blessed are you, Lord God of all creation . . .'

The familiar signs and symbols of the Eucharist take on new depths of meaning when we share the uplifting experience of a Maundy Thursday Passover celebration. That Last Supper Jesus ate with his disciples is suddenly seen in the context of God's saving love stretching from creation over the whole course of human history. As Christians we share common roots with our Jewish brothers and sisters, and the festival of Passover is part of our shared faith heritage. So to celebrate the meal like this together is a wonderful opportunity to discover a fresh way of telling the story of God's love, and finding it to be our own story.

The traditional order, or Seder, of this special evening takes place in the home, by candlelight, with family and friends around the table. It tells the profound story of the people's slavery in Egypt and their God rescuing them. The story is told through tastes and textures, prayers, readings and songs, the drinking of four cups of wine / grape juice, the breaking of bread, the eating of specially prepared food, and, through questions asked by the children, about what the meal means. The occasion is full of thanksgiving and praise as we remember God's love and care, but also full of empathy with the suffering of all who are oppressed and in great need. Rather than being simply a festive meal built on memories, the experience brings those saving events right into the present, binding the community together as children of God, reliving their escape in the presence of their Creator and Redeemer.

So both Jews and Christians meet with God in the simple act of sharing a cup of wine and a piece of bread together, full of thankfulness and praise for the One who made us, provides for us, and rescues us. And of course it was during a Seder meal that Jesus spoke of his own life being broken and poured out to save us from the slavery of sin. The bittersweet tastes of the Passover are there too in our Eucharist, as we thank God for saving us, yet know it to be through Jesus' costly suffering. We rejoice in the way we have been set free, yet at the same time hunger for the whole world to know that freedom.

Preparations for Passover

Have a good clear-out of the church hall before the meal, paying particular attention to anything which has been sitting there for ages without being used. Traditionally this is the perfect time to distribute things we are no longer using to those who can make use of them!

Set the tables beautifully, with cloths and, if possible, real cutlery, glasses and dishes, rather than disposable ones. Each place setting will also need a finger bowl with water in it. Involve the children in preparing the place names and place mats (see pages 73-76), and arrange the table so that everyone can see the leader's section, which should feel central, rather than separate.

The buffet meal and all the special dishes are arranged in clusters on each stretch of table, so that everyone has access to the same kind of food. Wine and grape juice are placed at regular intervals around the table and one place is left empty.

For each group of six people you will need the following:
- candles and flowers
- a glass of salty water
- sprigs of parsley or another springtime herb
- dish of maror ('bitter herb' of slavery, such as horseradish sauce)
- dish of haroseth ('sweetness of freedom', a mixture of chopped or grated apples, raisins, finely chopped nuts and cinnamon, made into little balls with grape juice or wine and coated with chopped nuts; or you can use dates)
- a basket of matzo (unleavened bread)

At the leader's table you will need the following:
- a candlestick for at least two candles, and some matches
- a glass of salty water
- a beautiful plate containing the springtime herbs, the bitter herb (maror), the sweet stuff (haroseth), a lamb or chicken bone and a hard-boiled egg
- three squares of matzo (unleavened bread) under a napkin

The rest of the food for the buffet can be anything delicious, and it is served with the matzo, the haroseth and vegetables.

The Order of Service*

1. The candle lighting

The leader welcomes everyone to the Passover, which is a celebration of the way God rescues his people from slavery. Everyone is asked to keep silence as they get ready to receive God's blessing at this Passover meal.

A short time of silence

The leader lights the candles, saying:

> Blessed are you, Lord God of all creation.
> Of your goodness we have the gift of light to lighten our darkness.

The light is passed all around the tables until every candle in the room is lit. 'The Lord is my light' (Taizé) may be sung quietly. As this is happening the leader prays:

> May the brightness of these small lights
> remind us of the great light of your love
> which brings us joy and hope.
> **Blessed be God for ever!**

2. We say Grace

We fill our glasses and raise them as we pray:

> Blessed are you, Lord God of all creation.
> Through your goodness we have this wine to drink,
> fruit of the vine and work of human hands.
> **Blessed be God for ever!**

Everyone drinks their wine or grape juice and fills the glass again.

3. We wash our hands

As we wash our fingers in the bowl of water we pray:

> Blessed are you, Lord God of all creation.
> You alone can make us clean.
> You alone can make us holy.
> **Blessed be God for ever!**

(At the Last Supper it was not just hands that were washed, but feet as well.)

4. Eating a springtime herb

The leader dips some of the parsley into the salty water, saying:

> Blessed are you, Lord God of all creation.
> Each springtime, through your goodness,
> the earth brings forth plants and fruit,
> to renew the world we inhabit.
> **Blessed be God for ever!**

Everyone dips some parsley in salty water and eats it.

---

*An A5 eight-page photocopiable version can be found in the Appendix.

5. The bread-sharing

The leader picks up the three pieces of matzo, and puts aside half a piece for unexpected guests, saying:

> Blessed are you, Lord God of all creation.
> Through your goodness we have this bread to eat
> which earth has given and human hands have made.
> Let us always share our bread with the hungry.
> We remember now all those who are persecuted or poor.
> Next year may we and they be free.
> Our Passover cannot be complete until all God's people are free.
> **Blessed be God for ever!**
>
> This is the bread of pain and affliction
> which our ancestors ate in Egypt, when they were slaves,
> and which our oppressed brothers and sisters eat now.
> Take this, all of you, and eat it.

The leader shares the bread with those around, and everyone else shares the bread near them with one another, dipping it in the salty water of tears, remembering the poor and oppressed. The piece of bread put aside is now hidden, for the children to find later on.

Leader:

> Let one of the children open our door
> to show that we welcome all who are hungry,
> in body and in spirit.

One of the children opens the door wide.

All:

> Let all who hunger for bread and for freedom,
> for truth, and for inner peace,
> come and share the bread which our God provides for us.

6. The story

The children:

Why is this night different from all other nights?

Leader:

> Thank you for asking that question, children. It is always good to ask questions, and find out the answers. That way you will learn the story we share and understand the traditions we value.
>
> Tonight is different from all other nights because we are celebrating something amazing. Once our ancestors were slaves of Pharaoh in Egypt, and God rescued our people, bringing us out of slavery into the promise of freedom and redemption. Our terrible suffering was turned into a time of happiness and blessing.

Child:

Why do we eat only flat bread without yeast tonight?

> When Pharaoh let the people go they had to escape in a great hurry. They had no time to wait for their bread to rise, so they baked it flat, like the bread we are eating tonight.

Child:

Why do we eat bitter herbs tonight?

The bitter herbs remind us that life was bitter and sad for the people when they were oppressed as slaves in the land of Egypt. When we taste the bitter herbs we taste the bitterness of every person who is sad and oppressed, and longs to be free.

Child:

Why do we have the sweet stuff to eat?

The sweet stuff reminds us of the sweetness of freedom when God brought us out of slavery. It reminds us of the sweetness of God's goodness and love which always triumphs over evil.

Child:

Why do we eat parsley?

We have parsley because it reminds us of all the fresh green plants of springtime which bring fresh new life to the world each year. Our God loves us and looks after us, and that makes us happy.

Child:

Why do we dip our parsley and bread in salt water?

The salt water reminds us of tears which people cry when they are very sad. As we taste the salty water we remember the tears of the people when they were slaves, and the tears of everyone who is not free or at peace with God.

Child:

Why is there a lamb bone?

Because the people ate a lamb that last night in Egypt, just before they were rescued. They put its blood on their doorposts and so they were protected from the plague of death that night. This was the tenth and last plague before Pharaoh agreed to let Moses and the people go. Let us express our compassion for the Egyptians who suffered those plagues. They were our enemies, but still they were children of God and fellow human beings, and we feel sorry for all who suffer – whether they are friends or enemies.

As each plague is mentioned, everyone dips a finger in their wine and drips it on their plate to remember the suffering:

Blood . . . Frogs . . . Vermin . . . Flies . . . Cattle disease . . . Boils . . . Hailstones . . . Locusts . . . Darkness . . . Death of every firstborn.

Child:

Why are we taking so much trouble over this meal tonight – with clean cloths and candles and flowers and party food?

Because thanks to God's loving rescue, we have all been set free from slavery and sin! In spite of all the tears and sadness in our world there is lots and lots to thank God for, and we want to enjoy thanking him as well as we can for all he has done in our lives.

Blessed be God for ever!

Everyone drinks their wine or grape juice, and refills the glass.

Leader:

Now we are ready to enjoy the Passover meal!

All:

We'll taste the bitterness of pain and oppression
and the sweetness of hope and freedom.
We'll eat thankfully of all God's gifts
and rejoice that we can share this time
and this food together in God's company.

7. The meal

The meal is eaten.

8. Hide and seek

After the meal the children can search for the afikomen (the hidden piece of matzo) and the one who finds it is given a reward. This piece of bread is broken and shared out among everyone. The bread is held as the leader says:

This bread is broken and shared to remind us of the Passover lambs which were sacrificed and shared, to give the people strength for their journey ahead and protection from the plague of death.

Everyone eats the fragment of bread.

A song is sung, such as 'Our God is so great, so strong and so mighty', 'You shall go out with joy', 'Give me joy in my heart' or 'Jubilate everybody'.

9. Grace after the meal

Leader:

The Bible tells us that when you have eaten and are satisfied you shall thank the Lord our God for the good land which he has given you. We have eaten and are satisfied, so let us thank God now.

Everyone raises their glasses as they pray:

All:

O Lord our God, we praise you
and thank you for feeding us all in body and spirit.

Women and girls:

We thank you for the good earth
and its fruitfulness.

Men and boys:

We thank you for the friendship we have shared tonight
and for the loving kindness you shower on us each day.

All:

> We thank you for freeing us from slavery and sin
> through the gift of your forgiveness.
> We pray that all God's children may be freed
> from hatred and hunger, oppression and guilt,
> free to live contentedly in your love. Amen.

Everyone drinks their wine or grape juice

Leader:

> Let us go in God's peace.
> Peace for us and peace for all people in the world.
> No more war. No more oppression.
> Justice and peace for everyone.
> Let it be so. **Amen. Let it be so.**

Everyone sings 'Shalom, my friends' (Billington)

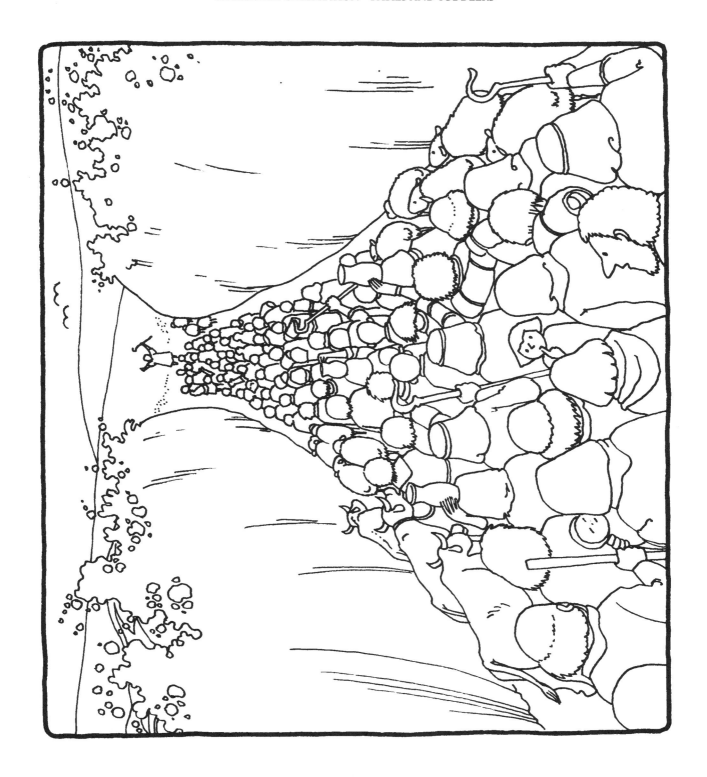

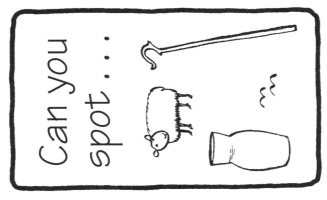

Can you spot . . . .

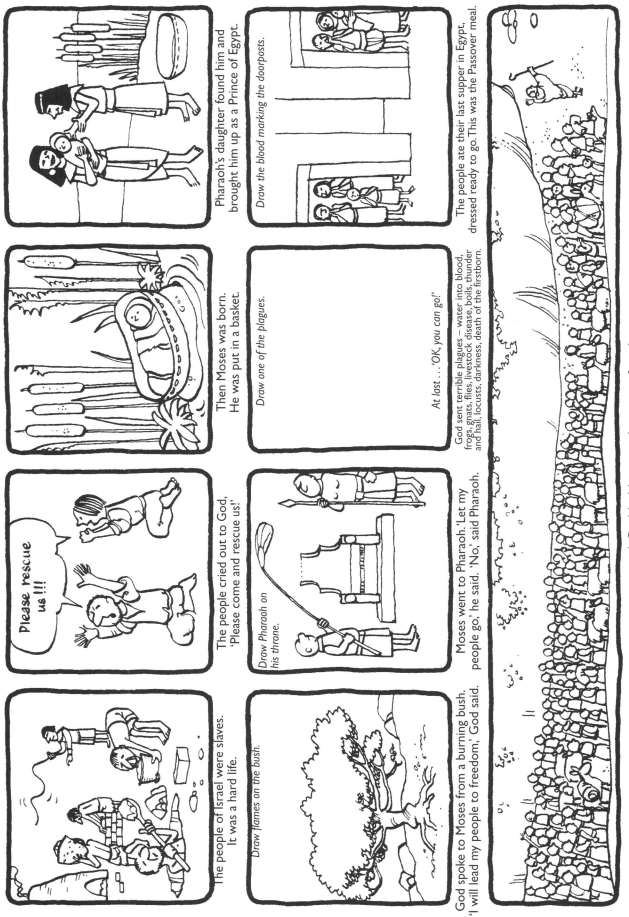

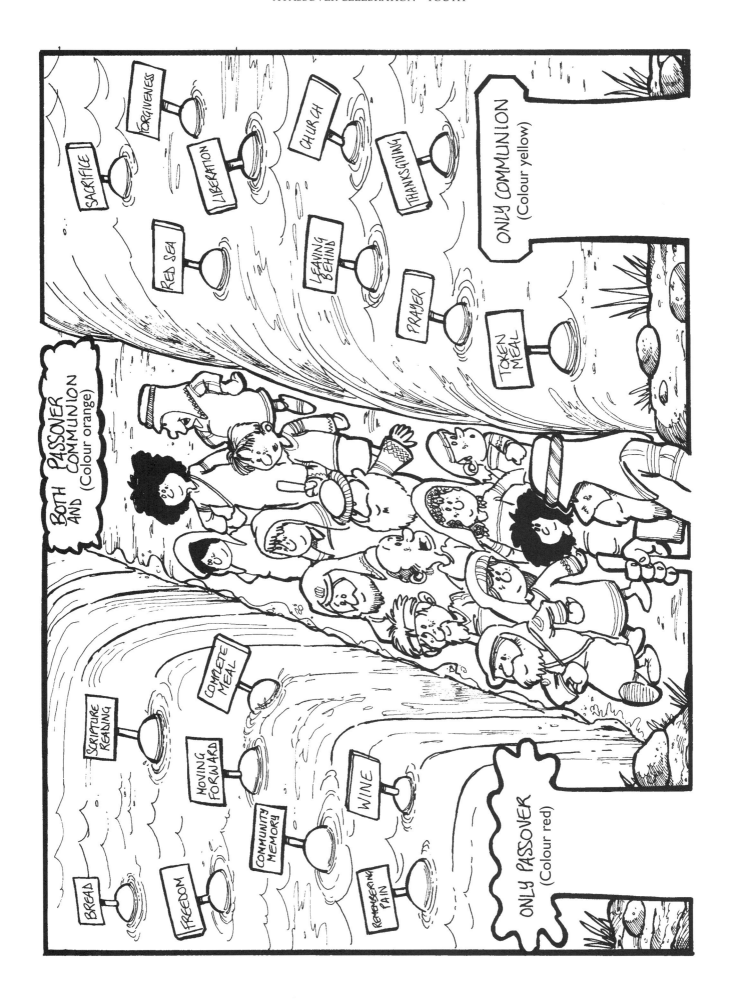

CONNECTIONS

CONNECTIONS

making

What kind of setting free?

What kind of setting free?

What animal's blood saved the people at Passover?

Any connections?

Why was the Passover a 'Last Supper'?

Why was the Last Supper a 'Passover'?

Think of the Passover

Think of the Last Supper

Telling the Good Friday story

'Truly this was the Son of God!'

Moving out of our churches on Good Friday to join in shared worship in our local areas is a powerful opportunity for mission and outreach. So many people have only a very vague idea of who Jesus is, and few would know why this Friday is called Good. For many, a telling of the Good Friday story as part of this worship will be a fresh event, and a 'churches together' story-telling will also give Christians the opportunity of hearing it in a new way.

Shared preparation

The idea is that, after processing through the town centre, everyone gathers in a public area, each person with a copy of the script. From within each church, groups take responsibility for preparing symbols and sound effects to be used, and in the telling all these sound effects and symbols are scattered throughout the gathering, so no one is far from them. People gather in small circles of up to 20 people, around a central space, like this:

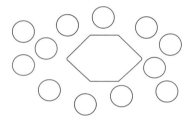

Advertise the event in the local press, inviting people to come to listen. They join the circles, so that there is at least one set of sound effects in each circle.

Symbols and sound effects

Each church brings one each of the following, prepared by different age groups. I have given suggestions for how the sounds might be made, but do use the ideas of the group to come up with whatever seems most effective.

- **The betrayal:** A pouch with 30 silver coins, which is shaken at the first * in the story (page 79), and then, at the second *, it is opened and the coins thrown out on the ground. (Coins can be made from card covered in foil, or you could use metal disks.)
- **The arrest:** The sound of metal clashing on metal (cutlery, metal umbrella spokes) and metal chains clinking. The sound of footsteps running (a flat bowl of gravel and blocks of wood stamped into them by several people at once). Shouts of soldiers.
- **Peter's denial:** The sound of a fire (crackling paper). The sound of a cock crowing (someone can make this sound).
- **Pilate washes his hands:** A bowl and a jug of water. Pour the water into the bowl and wash your hands in it noisily.

- **The flogging:** Whips of rope flung several times against the ground.
- **The crown of thorns:** Woven hawthorn or bramble (using thick gardening gloves) held up at the appropriate time and then placed in the centre of each circle of people.
- **The cross:** Two large pieces of wood and some rope which is used to lash them together. The sign 'Jesus of Nazareth, King of the Jews' is on a nail which is hammered in.
- **The crucifixion:** Nails are hammered into wood.
- **The dice:** Two big dice are made and rolled. (Cube boxes covered with paper, and spots stuck or painted on.)
- **The curtain of the temple:** Some heavy fabric, already cut to start off a rip. It is ripped strongly apart.
- **Earthquake:** Large metal tray or sheet of heavy card, rattled.

The story

Men and boys About 2000 years ago in Bethlehem, Jesus was born. When he was about 30 years old Jesus travelled for two or three years around the areas of Galilee and Jerusalem, announcing the kingdom of God.

Women and girls Many were healed by him, many forgiven, and many given new hope in God because of what Jesus said and did.

All **Huge crowds would seek him out wherever he went, and Jesus was well known for his compassion and his wisdom. He was also well known for speaking out the truth, even when the truth wasn't comfortable to hear. That made him enemies as well as followers.**

A man Jesus had gathered a group of twelve disciples and trained them. Judas, one of these close friends, went to the Roman authorities and offered to betray Jesus to them. They paid him thirty pieces of silver for the information. * After Jesus' death Judas was horrified by what he had done, and threw the money down at their feet before committing suicide. *

A woman Another of Jesus' disciples, called Peter, had promised Jesus he would never let him down or desert him, whatever happened. But Jesus had looked at him and told him that before the cock crowed, Peter would have denied him three times.

A child Peter was sure Jesus was wrong about that.

All **Led by Judas, the soldiers found Jesus praying among the olive trees in the darkness of Thursday evening. Judas greeted Jesus with a kiss, to show the soldiers which one he was, and they arrested him. * All Jesus' disciples ran away.**

Men and boys	The soldiers dragged him before Caiaphas, the High Priest, to face his accusers. They were all making false statements against him. Peter crept into the courtyard to find out what was happening. It was cold, and there was a fire burning there. *
Peter	As Peter stood getting warm by the fire, a servant girl came out and said:
A woman	'You also were with Jesus the Galilean.'
Peter	Peter denied it. 'I don't know what you're talking about!' he said. Another servant girl noticed him and told the bystanders:
A woman	'This man here was with Jesus of Nazareth!'
Peter	Peter denied it again. 'I swear I don't know the man!' he said. Then one of the bystanders came up to him.
A man	'You certainly are one of them – your accent gives you away!'
Peter	Peter swore blind that he didn't know Jesus at all. And just then the cock crowed,* and Jesus turned his head and looked straight at him. Peter suddenly remembered his promise, and what Jesus had said, and he felt terrible. He went out into the darkness, broke down and wept bitterly.
Women and girls	Those who were holding Jesus were mocking him. Jesus had a reputation for being a prophet, so they blindfolded him and then hit him, calling out:
Men and boys	'Go on, Prophet, prophesy! Who is it who struck you that time?'
Women and girls	On Friday morning they brought Jesus to the Council, and started questioning him.
A man	'If you are the Messiah, then tell us.'

Jesus	Jesus replied, 'If I tell you, you won't believe me. But I'll give you a clue – from now on the Son of Man will be seated at the right hand of God.'
All	**At that, all of them started asking, 'So you are the Son of God, then?'**
Jesus	Jesus was careful how he replied. He said, 'You say that I am.'
All	**'That settles it,' they said. 'What other evidence do we need? We've heard it from his own lips!' And they brought Jesus to the Roman governor of the time – Pontius Pilate.**
Pilate	When Pilate heard Jesus was from the Galilee region, he sent him off to Herod. Herod and his soldiers treated Jesus with contempt and sent him back to Pilate. But Pilate could find no offence he was guilty of, because Jesus was innocent. The crowds were all shouting for Jesus' death.
All	**'Crucify him! Crucify him!'**
Pilate	Pilate could see a riot was brewing, which was the last thing he wanted. He took some water * and in full sight of the crowds he washed his hands, shouting, 'I am innocent of the blood of this just man. See to it yourselves!' He had Jesus flogged * and then handed him over for death by crucifixion.
Men and boys	The soldiers stripped Jesus and put a scarlet robe on him, pushing a crown made of thorns * down over his head. They put a reed in his hand and pretended to bow down as if to a king, saying 'Hail, O King of the Jews!' And they spat on him and hit him.
Women and girls	Then Jesus was led away through the streets of Jerusalem, staggering from the beatings

and carrying the cross* for his own execution. When he had fallen a couple of times they made a visitor to the city help carry the cross. All along the way the crowds watched him pass. Some were jeering at him, some crying. His mother was there, helpless.

Men and boys They went out of the city to a hill called The Scull, where they nailed* Jesus to the cross by his hands and feet, and hoisted the cross into a slot in the rock so it stood upright. The soldiers threw dice* to win his clothes, and then they sat down to watch him die. The charge against him was fixed above his head:

All **'Jesus of Nazareth, King of the Jews.'**

A few men That didn't please the High Priests at all. They said, 'The whole point is that he pretended to be the King of the Jews – and that's blasphemy, punishable by death!' But no one changed the sign.

All **People passing by would call out, 'He saved others, but he can't save himself, can he?' or 'Come down from that cross – then we'll believe you!'**

Jesus Jesus was praying, 'Father, forgive them – they don't understand what they're doing.'

Men and boys On either side of Jesus were bandits, also being crucified to death. One of them was cursing him, but the other asked, 'Lord, remember me when you come into your kingdom.'

Jesus And Jesus said to him, 'I promise you, this very day you will be with me in Paradise!'

Women and girls When it got to midday, there was darkness over the whole country for three hours, and at three o'clock in the afternoon Jesus cried out with a loud voice:

Jesus 'Father, into your hands I commend my spirit!' And he breathed his last, and died.

All   **And the curtain to the holy of holies in the temple was suddenly ripped in two,* from the top to the bottom, and the earth shook and rocks were split apart. ***

Centurion   When the centurion saw the way Jesus died, he said, 'Truly this man was God's Son.'

Men and boys   The soldiers came to speed up the dying by breaking the legs of the people being crucified, but when they came to Jesus he was already dead – they checked by piercing his side and found the blood had already separated into the blood and water of death.

Women and girls   Many women were there, watching from a distance, and Joseph of Arimathea, a rich man, and a disciple of Jesus, asked the authorities for the body.

Men and boys   Joseph took the body of Jesus down from the cross, wrapped it in a clean linen cloth and laid it in his new tomb in the rock. A great stone was rolled across the entrance to seal it.

All   **So Jesus was laid to rest on Friday evening, as the Sabbath was beginning.**

A child   But death could not hold the Lord of life. By Sunday, Jesus was alive again in a whole new way, and he has been alive ever since.

All   **We believe that Jesus, who died on the cross that day, is the Son of God, and we worship him as Lord and Saviour. Amen.**

Appendix

The stone soup story

Once upon a time a stranger was travelling far from home. He was tired and hungry, and at last he came to a village. He knocked at the door of a cottage and a well-dressed woman opened it. 'What do you want?' she asked suspiciously.

'I am weary with travel, said the stranger, and I would be grateful for some food.'

'We haven't got enough food for ourselves,' she said. And she shut the door in his face.

The stranger walked on and tried another house where there were lots of ragged children playing and fighting. Their father looked out at the stranger. 'There is not enough food for my own children,' he said, and turned his back on the man.

So it went on until the stranger reached the middle of the village. No one was willing to share their food with him.

Then the stranger had an idea. On the village green he lit a fire and took from his back the cooking pot he carried. He found a large, smooth stone and put it in the bottom of the cooking pot. He filled the pot with water from the stream and set it on the fire to boil.

The people from the village were very curious, and came across to watch what this stranger was doing. 'What are you cooking?' they asked.

'Oh, it's my favourite supper,' said the stranger. 'It's stone soup, and it's delicious!'

The water was beginning to bubble now, and the stranger stirred it and sniffed it. 'Mmmm! This is going to be the best stone soup I've ever cooked!' he said, 'and you're all welcome to share it.'

One of the women came up. 'That stone soup might be even better with a few onions in it,' she said, and went off home to get some.

'I reckon it needs a few carrots,' said an old man, chopping some up and throwing them in.

'Is stone soup nice with swedes and turnips?' asked the man with all the children, 'because if so you can have these!' And he and the children chopped up their swedes and turnips and threw them in the pot.

A young couple brought some chopped potatoes and an old couple brought some herbs and salt and pepper.

The stranger kept stirring the soup and at last he said, 'It's ready!'

Everyone in the village sat around on the grass with their bowls, and the stranger poured out stone soup for them all. And they all ate and chatted and laughed together, and agreed it was the best soup they'd ever tasted!

Growing together

Jesus explained lots of things to the people in stories. 'Listen to this!' he'd say. 'Don't let it go in one ear and out of the other – really listen to it so you hear with your heart as well as your ears!' And this is one of the stories he told.

'A farmer went out sowing seed. As he was scattering the seeds, some fell on the path, and the birds swooped down and ate them, so they didn't grow at all. Some of the seeds fell where the ground was rocky, so the young shoots grew fast all right, but they wilted and died away as soon as the strong sun burnt down on them. That's because they hadn't had room to grow a strong root system in the shallow earth. Some other seeds fell in the middle of where the thorns and weeds were growing. Weeds grow faster and stronger than wheat, and they choked the young shoots so they died away. But other seeds fell in the right place, in the good, rich earth prepared for them, so that they grew up strong and tall, and yielded a good crop – 100 per cent, 60 per cent or 30 per cent increase on what had been sown.
Based on Matthew 13:3-9

This Lent we are all going to grow a plant, taking care of it and watering it. Then we'll bring the plants to church in the week before Easter, and they will all become part of a special Easter garden. Keep this leaflet next to your plant and read it every day.

A daily growing prayer

Lord Jesus,
may your kingdom grow in us
and may your will be done.
Amen.

29. I treasure your word in my heart, so that I may not sin against you. *Psalm 119:11*

30. The Lord is your keeper; the Lord is your shade at your right hand. The sun shall not strike you by day, nor the moon by night. *Psalm 121:5, 6*

31. With the Lord there is steadfast love, and with him is great power to redeem. *Psalm 130:7*

32. O Lord, you have searched me and known me, you know when I sit down and when I rise up . . . you search out my path and my lying down, and are familiar with all my ways. *Psalm 139:1-3*

33. Set a guard over my mouth, O Lord; keep watch over the door of my lips. *Psalm 141:3*

34. My eyes are turned towards you, O God, my Lord; in you I seek refuge. *Psalm 141:8*

35. Let me hear of your steadfast love in the morning, for in you I put my trust. Teach me the way I should go, for to you I lift up my soul. *Psalm 143:8*

36. The Lord is gracious and merciful, slow to anger and abounding in steadfast love. The Lord is good to all, and his compassion is over all that he has made. *Psalm 145:8, 9*

37. The Lord is just in all his ways, and kind in all his doings. The Lord is near to all who call on him, to all who call on him in truth. *Psalm 145:17, 18*

38. The Lord sets the prisoners free; the Lord opens the eyes of the blind. The Lord lifts up those who are bowed down. *Psalm 146:8*

39. The Lord heals the broken-hearted and binds up their wounds. *Psalm 147:3*

40. Praise him, sun and moon; praise him all you shining stars! Let them praise the Lord for he commanded and they were created. *Psalm 148:3, 5*

Let everything that has breath praise the Lord! Alleluia!
Psalm 150:6

Forty daily readings from the Psalms to help the kingdom grow in you

1. You show me the path of life. In your presence there is fullness of joy. *Psalm 16:11*

2. It is you who light my lamp; the Lord my God lights up my darkness. *Psalm 18:28*

3. The Lord is my shepherd; there is nothing else I need. *Psalm 23:1*

4. To you, O Lord, I lift up my soul. O my God, in you I trust. *Psalm 25:1, 2*

5. Make me to know your ways, O Lord; teach me your paths. *Psalm 25:4*

6. All the paths of the Lord are steadfast love and faithfulness. *Psalm 25:10*

7. Keep your tongue from evil and your lips from speaking lies. Depart from evil and do good. Psalm 34:13, 14

8. Be still before the Lord and wait patiently for him. *Psalm 37:7*

9. Depart from evil and do good; so you shall abide for ever. For the Lord loves justice; he will not forsake his faithful ones. *Psalm 37:27, 28*

10. I waited patiently for the Lord; he leaned over to me and heard my cry. He drew me up from the desolate pit, out of the muddy swamp, and set my feet upon a rock, making my steps secure. *Psalm 40:1, 2*

11. As the deer longs for flowing streams, so my soul longs for you, O God. My soul thirsts for God, for the living God. *Psalm 42:1*

12. Why are you cast down, O my soul, and why are you disquieted within me? Hope in God; for I shall again praise him, my help and my God. Psalm 42:11

13. Be still and know that I am God! *Psalm 46:10*

14. For you have been my help, and in the shadow of your wings I sing for joy. *Psalm 63:7*

15. Glorious are you, more majestic than the everlasting mountains. *Psalm 76:4*

16. I cry aloud to God that he may hear me. In the day of my trouble I seek the Lord. *Psalm 77:1, 2*

17. Things that we have heard and known, that our ancestors have told us, we will not hide them from their children; we will tell to the coming generation the glorious deeds of the Lord . . . and the wonders he has done. *Psalm 78:3, 4*

18. Happy is everyone who trusts in you. *Psalm 84:12*

19. For you, O Lord, are good and forgiving. *Psalm 86:5*

20. You are merciful and gracious, slow to anger and of great faithfulness. *Psalm 86:15*

21. The heavens are yours, the earth also is yours; the world and all that is in it – you have created them. *Psalm 89:11*

22. Before the mountains were born, before you had formed the earth and the world, from everlasting to everlasting you are God. *Psalm 90:2*

23. For a thousand years in your sight are like yesterday when it is past . . . *Psalm 90:4*

24. O come, let us worship and bow down, let us kneel before the Lord our Maker! For he is our God and we are the people of his pasture, and the sheep of his hand. *Psalm 95:6, 7*

25. Bless the Lord, O my soul, and all that is within me, bless his holy name. *Psalm 103:1*

26. He turns a desert into pools of water, a parched land into springs of water. *Psalm 107:35*

27. He raises the poor from the dust, and lifts the needy from the ash heap. *Psalm 113:7*

28. Out of my distress I called on the Lord; he answered me and set me in a broad place. With the Lord at my side I do not fear. *Psalm 118:5, 6*

Men and boys:

We thank you for the friendship we have shared tonight and for the loving kindness you shower on us each day.

All:

We thank you for freeing us from slavery and sin through the gift of your forgiveness.
We pray that all God's children may be freed from hatred and hunger, oppression and guilt, free to live contentedly in your love. Amen.

Everyone drinks their wine or grape juice

Leader:

Let us go in God's peace.
Peace for us and peace for all people in the world.
No more war. No more oppression.
Justice and peace for everyone.
Let it be so. **Amen. Let it be so.**

Everyone sings 'Shalom, my friends'

A Passover
Celebration

Order of service

1. The candle lighting

The leader welcomes everyone to the Passover, which is a celebration of the way God rescues his people from slavery. Everyone is asked to keep silence as they get ready to receive God's blessing at this Passover meal.

A short time of silence

The leader lights the candles, saying:

Blessed are you, Lord God of all creation.
Of your goodness we have the gift of light
to lighten our darkness.

The light is passed all around the tables until every candle in the room is lit. 'The Lord is my light' (Taizé) may be sung quietly. As this is happening the leader prays:

May the brightness of these small lights
remind us of the great light of your love
which brings us joy and hope.
Blessed be God for ever!

2. We say Grace

We fill our glasses and raise them as we pray:

Blessed are you, Lord God of all creation.
Through your goodness we have this wine to drink,
fruit of the vine and work of human hands.
Blessed be God for ever!

Everyone drinks their wine or grape juice and fills the glass again.

3. We wash our hands

As we wash our fingers in the bowl of water we pray:

7. The meal

The meal is eaten.

8. Hide and seek

After the meal the children can search for the afikomen (the hidden piece of matzo) and the one who finds it is given a reward. This piece of bread is broken and shared out among everyone. The bread is held as the leader says:

This bread is broken and shared to remind us of the Passover lambs which were sacrificed and shared, to give the people strength for their journey ahead and protection from the plague of death.

Everyone eats the fragment of bread.

A song is sung, such as 'Our God is so great, so strong and so mighty', 'You shall go out with joy', 'Give me joy in my heart' or 'Jubilate everybody'.

9. Grace after the meal

Leader:

The Bible tells us that when you have eaten and are satisfied you shall thank the Lord our God for the good land which he has given you. We have eaten and are satisfied, so let us thank God now.

Everyone raises their glasses as they pray:

All:

O Lord our God, we praise you
and thank you for feeding us all in body and spirit.

Women and girls:

We thank you for the good earth
and its fruitfulness.

Blessed are you, Lord God of all creation.
You alone can make us clean.
You alone can make us holy.
Blessed be God for ever!

(At the Last Supper it was not just hands that were washed, but feet as well.)

4. Eating a springtime herb

The leader dips some of the parsley into the salty water, saying:

Blessed are you, Lord God of all creation.
Each springtime, through your goodness,
the earth brings forth plants and fruit,
to renew the world we inhabit.
Blessed be God for ever!

Everyone dips some parsley in salty water and eats it.

5. The bread-sharing

The leader picks up the three pieces of matzo, and puts aside half a piece for unexpected guests, saying:

Blessed are you, Lord God of all creation.
Through your goodness we have this bread to eat
which earth has given and human hands have made.
Let us always share our bread with the hungry.
We remember now all those who are persecuted or poor.
Next year may we and they be free.
Our Passover cannot be complete
until all God's people are free.
Blessed be God for ever!

This is the bread of pain and affliction
which our ancestors ate in Egypt, when they were slaves,
and which our oppressed brothers and sisters eat now.
Take this, all of you, and eat it.

that night. This was the tenth and last plague before Pharaoh agreed to let Moses and the people go. Let us express our compassion for the Egyptians who suffered those plagues. They were our enemies, but still they were children of God and fellow human beings, and we feel sorry for all who suffer – whether they are friends or enemies.

As each plague is mentioned, everyone dips a finger in their wine and drips it on their plate to remember the suffering:

Blood . . . Frogs . . . Vermin . . . Flies . . . Cattle disease . . . Boils . . . Hailstones . . . Locusts . . . Darkness . . . Death of every firstborn.

Child:

Why are we taking so much trouble over this meal tonight – with clean cloths and candles and flowers and party food?

Because thanks to God's loving rescue, we have all been set free from slavery and sin! In spite of all the tears and sadness in our world there is lots and lots to thank God for, and we want to enjoy thanking him as well as we can for all he has done in our lives.
Blessed be God for ever!

Everyone drinks their wine or grape juice, and refills the glass.

Leader:
Now we are ready to enjoy the Passover meal!

All:
We'll taste the bitterness of pain and oppression
and the sweetness of hope and freedom.
We'll eat thankfully of all God's gifts
and rejoice that we can share this time
and this food together in God's company.

The leader shares the bread with those around, and everyone else shares the bread near them with one another, dipping it in the salty water of tears, remembering the poor and oppressed. The piece of bread put aside is now hidden, for the children to find later on.

Leader:

Let one of the children open our door
to show that we welcome all who are hungry,
in body and in spirit.

One of the children opens the door wide.

All:

Let all who hunger for bread and for freedom,
for truth, and for inner peace,
come and share the bread which our God provides for us.

6. The story

The children:

Why is this night different from all other nights?

Leader:

Thank you for asking that question, children. It is always good to ask questions, and find out the answers. That way you will learn the story we share and understand the traditions we value.

Tonight is different from all other nights because we are celebrating something amazing. Once our ancestors were slaves of Pharaoh in Egypt, and God rescued our people, bringing us out of slavery into the promise of freedom and redemption. Our terrible suffering was turned into a time of happiness and blessing.

Child:

Why do we eat only flat bread without yeast tonight?

When Pharaoh let the people go they had to escape in a great hurry. They had no time to wait for their bread to rise, so they baked it flat, like the bread we are eating tonight.

Child:

Why do we eat bitter herbs tonight?

The bitter herbs remind us that life was bitter and sad for the people when they were oppressed as slaves in the land of Egypt. When we taste the bitter herbs we taste the bitterness of every person who is sad and oppressed, and longs to be free.

Child:

Why do we have the sweet stuff to eat?

The sweet stuff reminds us of the sweetness of freedom when God brought us out of slavery. It reminds us of the sweetness of God's goodness and love which always triumphs over evil.

Child:

Why do we eat parsley?

We have parsley because it reminds us of all the fresh green plants of springtime which bring fresh new life to the world each year. Our God loves us and looks after us, and that makes us happy.

Child:

Why do we dip our parsley and bread in salt water?

The salt water reminds us of tears which people cry when they are very sad. As we taste the salty water we remember the tears of the people when they were slaves, and the tears of everyone who is not free or at peace with God.

Child:

Why is there a lamb bone?

Because the people ate a lamb that last night in Egypt, just before they were rescued. They put its blood on their doorposts and so they were protected from the plague of death

Acknowledgements

The publishers are grateful to the following for permission to reproduce their copyright material:

The Beatitudes (page 47) from *Matthew for Everyone, Part 1* by Tom Wright, Copyright © 2002 SPCK, Holy Trinity Church, Marylebone Road, London, NW1 4DU. Used by permission.

Scripture quotations are taken from the following versions of the Bible:

New International Version. Copyright © 1973, 1978, 1984 by International Bible Society. Used by permission of Hodder & Stoughton, a division of Hodder Headline Ltd. All rights reserved.

New Revised Standard Version. Copyright © 1989 by the Division of Christian Education of the National Council of Churches of Christ in the USA. Used by permission. All rights reserved.

The Message. Copyright © 1993, 1994, 1995, 1996, 2000, 2001, 2002 by Eugene H. Peterson. Used by permission of NavPress Publishing Group.

International Children's Bible ®. Copyright © 1986, 1988, 1999 by Tommy Nelson™, a division of Thomas Nelson, Inc. Used by permission. All rights reserved.